Ma

heatre & the rural

Theatre &
Series Editors: Jen Harvie and Dan Rebellato

Published
Joel Anderson: *Theatre & Photography*
Susan Bennett: *Theatre & Museums*
Bill Blake: *Theatre & the Digital*
Colette Conroy: *Theatre & the Body*
Emma Cox: *Theatre & Migration*
Jim Davis: *Theatre & Entertainment*
Jill Dolan: *Theatre & Sexuality*
Helen Freshwater: *Theatre & Audience*
Jen Harvie: *Theatre & the City*
Nadine Holdsworth: *Theatre & Nation*
Erin Hurley: *Theatre & Feeling*
Dominic Johnson: *Theatre & the Visual*
Joe Kelleher: *Theatre & Politics*
Ric Knowles: *Theatre & Interculturalism*
Patrick Lonergan: *Theatre & Social Media*
Caoimhe McAvinchey: *Theatre & Prison*
Bruce McConachie: *Theatre & Mind*
Lucy Nevitt: *Theatre & Violence*
Helen Nicholson: *Theatre & Education*
Lourdes Orozco: *Theatre & Animals*
Lionel Pilkington: *Theatre & Ireland*
Benjamin Poore: *Theatre & Empire*
Paul Rae: *Theatre & Human Rights*
Alan Read: *Theatre & Law*
Dan Rebellato: *Theatre & Globalization*
Trish Reid: *Theatre & Scotland*
Nicholas Ridout: *Theatre & Ethics*
Jo Robinson: *Theatre & the Rural*
Juliet Rufford: *Theatre & Architecture*
Rebecca Schneider: *Theatre & History*
Kim Solga: *Theatre & Feminism*
Fintan Walsh: *Theatre & Therapy*
Eric Weitz: *Theatre & Laughter*
David Wiles: *Theatre & Time*
Harvey Young: *Theatre & Race*

Forthcoming
Keren Zaiontz: *Theatre & Festivals*
Lara Shalson: *Theatre & Protest*
Paul Murphy: *Theatre & Class*

Matt Delbridge: *Theatre & Technology*
Konstantinos Thomaidis: *Theatre & Voice*

Theatre&
Series Standing Order ISBN 978–0–230–20327–3

You can receive future titles in this series as they are published by placing a standing order. Please contact your bookseller or, in case of difficulty, write to us at the address below with your name and address, the title of the series and the ISBN quoted above.

Customer Services Department, Macmillan Distribution Ltd, Houndmills, Basingstoke, Hampshire, RG21 6XS, UK

theatre &
the rural

Jo Robinson

 macmillan
education   palgrave

First published 2016 by
PALGRAVE

Palgrave in the UK is an imprint of Macmillan Publishers Limited, registered in England, company number 785998, of 4 Crinan Street, London, N1 9XW.

Palgrave Macmillan in the US is a division of St Martin's Press LLC, 175 Fifth Avenue, New York, NY 10010.

Palgrave is a global imprint of the above companies and is represented throughout the world.

Palgrave® and Macmillan® are registered trademarks in the United States, the United Kingdom, Europe and other countries.

ISBN 978–1–137–47193–2 paperback

This book is printed on paper suitable for recycling and made from fully managed and sustained forest sources. Logging, pulping and manufacturing processes are expected to conform to the environmental regulations of the country of origin.

A catalogue record for this book is available from the British Library.

A catalog record for this book is available from the Library of Congress.

Printed in China

For Nick, Justin and Ella

contents

Foreword   ix

Introduction   1

   Rural ideal/rural reality   3

   Rural representations   4

   Viewing the rural   7

Defining the rural   9

   A rural sense of place   12

   Rural nostalgias   18

Performing the rural   20

   Rural freedoms, rural exiles   26

   Rural as other: from *Roots* to Rudkin and beyond   31

   The rural as the nation   38

   Rural stories, rural radicals   44

The place of performance   51

The rural as site for performance   53

From the centre to the rural: theatre for rural
development   59

Rural touring theatre   63

Performing the local rural: New Perspectives
as case study   68

Defining new nationals through theatre:
including the rural   73

Conclusion   78

Further reading   81

Index   88

Acknowledgements   91

foreword

In October 1995, Welsh theatre company Brith Gof staged *Tri Bywyd* (*Three Lives*) at Esgair Fraith, a ruined farmhouse in the coniferous Clywedog plantation, east of Lampeter (see p. 58, this volume). Here, director Cliff McLucas erected two large scaffolding structures, creating three interlocking architectures in which to situate parallel narratives. Taking the original occupation as a datum, one was of period but not place – the fate of Sarah Jacobs, the 'fasting girl of Llandysul', who in 1869 was not seen to eat for two years and who eventually died under the concerted gaze of nurses from Guy's Hospital. A second was of place but not period – a fictional account of contemporary rural bankruptcy and suicide. And a third was of neither place nor period – the killing of Cardiff prostitute Lynette White in 1988. The site itself was redolent of upland depopulation and the industrialisation of landscape, the sophisticated design – with neon lighting and amplified soundtrack – startling in such an infrequently visited location.

One withering newspaper review (*Independent*, 20 October 1995) reveals many of the attitudes and perceptions *Theatre & the Rural* so successfully challenges and counters. The critic effectively casts the rural as distant and backward, *Tri Bywyd* occurring 'somewhere in darkest Wales'. At Aberystwyth Arts Centre, 'buses arrive to take us to another – even more remote – place'. Once aboard, a fellow traveller remarks: '"I've got a new hammer", "Anyone like to see it?" "Ooh yes," reply two women to my right. "Heavy, isn't it", "Show it to Meddie [sic] James. She likes hammers".' And as alien and exclusive: 'I had been worried the play might be in Welsh'; 'I'd been eyed with vague suspicion'. The reviewer's critique is damning, the production 'a prolonged travesty of movement and sound'; '. . . the tawdrily overbearing soundtrack from some am-dram production of The Woman in Black'. In comparison, one wonders, to what, here at a place of desertion and dereliction. Where a community gathers once more, their momentary congress as affective as the aesthetic efforts on display. Where the labour of artistic production in extreme circumstances is evident and redolent of past efforts at dwelling. His excitement at the presence of a dead sheep hints at national stereotyping, yet he worries that its symbolism is 'never explained'. As if performance here – where whole flocks perished in the snows of March 2013, driving hill farmers to despair – cannot generate resonant imagery based on specifically regional cultural experiences. Ultimately, he finds solace in the collective experience of audience: 'We are subdued and a little outraged'. But he will return to the city, and it is the rest of that 'we' who, in Raymond Williams words, will await 'discovery and recovery from the fallacy of idiocy'. Herein lies *Theatre & the Rural*'s quest. . .

theatre & the rural

Introduction

> Cormoran. Woden. Jack-of-Green. Jack-in-
> Irons. Thunderdell. Búri, Blunderbore, Gog
> and Magog, Galligantus. Vili and Vé, Yggdrasil,
> Brutus of Albion. Come, you drunken spirits.
> Come, you battalions. You fields of ghosts who
> walk these green plains still. Come, you giants!
> (Jez Butterworth, *Jerusalem*, 2009, p. 109)

Johnny 'Rooster' Byron's rallying cry, accompanied by the
relentless beating of his drum, brought Jez Butterworth's
2009 *Jerusalem* to its close on the stage of London's Royal
Court theatre with an invocation of the still talismanic
power of England's green spaces – of the 'pleasant pas-
tures', 'mountains green' and 'clouded hills' of William
Blake's poem which gives the play its name. Butterworth's
play brought to the stage two versions of the rural, as Laura

1

Barton identified in the *Guardian*: 'the country we recognise, scruffed right up against that dreamy, idealised place of popular imagination – that scepter'd, green, and pleasant land, stewed with an island that is squat and gristly and fierce' ('Why I love Jez Butterworth's Jerusalem', *Guardian*, 25 October 2011). In other words, for every Rooster, whose character seemed to Barton to contain resonances of 'Robin Hood, Will o' the Wisp, Puck, John Barleycorn, the Green Man, [and] George and the Dragon', Butterworth also provides a Davey, working in the abattoir: 'Get there six in the morning – hungover, hazmat suit, goggles – and I stand there and I slay two hundred cows. [...] Have lunch. Pot Noodle. Come back. Slay two hundred more' (p. 89).

Jerusalem brought to the London stage a complex, double-edged experience of the rural. Its audiences were confronted both with the proscenium adorned with cherubs and woodland scenes and the '*Rubbish. Empty bottles. A car seat, a swing [... and] the remains of a smashed television*' scattered around the woodland clearing. Their experience thus mirrored the unexpected reality facing the residents of the 'seventy-eight brand new houses' on the nearby estate mentioned in the play:

> DAVEY   I bet it never said in the brochure: 'Detached house, three beds with garden overlooking wood with free troll. Free ogre what loves trance music, deals cheap spliff and whizz, don't pay no tax, and has probably got

AIDS. Guaranteed non-stop aggra-
vation and danger.' I bet that weren't
in the brochure. (p. 30)

Rural ideal/rural reality

With its contrasts between the ancient landscapes of pre-
historic England and the encroaching houses of the new
estate, David Rabey suggests that Butterworth's play
raises a wider set of questions about English society and
culture: questions 'about belonging and corporate power
and local control and who is in charge; about a sense of
place and what constitutes it' (2015, pp. 108–9, citing
Kingsnorth, 2008, p. 106). Those questions run urgently
through this volume, and through my discussion of theatre
that both represents a rural sense of place and plays a part
in constituting it. The next section of this book, 'Defining
the rural', thus begins with an interrogation of that rural
sense of place, and the freight of imagery that it carries.
While acknowledging that the rural is multiple and varied,
woven into the different elements of the increasingly complex relationships between the different countries, regions
and communities that make up the United Kingdom, I
argue that there is a tendency to persistently return to a
nostalgic and idealised perspective of the rural as a 'green
world'. As the Marxist critic and key twentieth-century
cultural thinker Raymond Williams recognised in his
seminal discussion of *The Country and the City* (1973):
'on the country' – what I am terming 'the rural' in this
book – 'has gathered the idea of a natural way of life: of

peace, innocence and simple virtue' as well as 'backwardness, ignorance, limitation', even though 'the real history,
throughout, has been astonishingly varied' (p. 1).

Using the framework of French philosopher and soci-
ologist Henri Lefebvre's three-fold understanding of space
as perceived, conceived and lived, through which he argues
that space is always produced rather than natural and neu-
tral, I argue in 'Defining the rural' that the reality of the
lived rural is frequently overlaid with external representations and perceptions, which can shape the potential of
rural lives. Indeed, it is partly the aim of this volume to
explore the ways in which theatre has had and might have a
role to play in the cultural production of such perceptions.
But I also argue that, setting aside such perceptions, we
need to re-engage with the actual place and lived practices of the rural in order to fully understand the nations
that we live in or visit. Thus, while the examples here are
largely taken from a UK or Irish context, the questions
raised will resonate in other countries and nations, wherever divisions between urban and rural exist.

Rural representations

The implications of our repeated failure to fully engage
with the rural in all its guises are problematic, as Christine
Hamilton and Adrienne Scullion make clear in *The Same, but
Different*, their 2004 report on rural arts touring in Scotland:

> we must be aware of a broader cultural tendency
> to see the rural [...] as a romanticised space, a

> magical and uncanny space. If we continually
> cast the rural in this way – without countering
> it with a more pragmatic reading – then we also
> romanticise rural policies and strategic solutions
> that emerge from rural areas. (p. 20)

Through the discussion of theatre and the rural in this book, I want to suggest that theatre and performance offer a space and a stage through which different visions of the rural can be explored, countered and critiqued. Indeed, despite what I identify below in 'Performing the rural' as theatre's persistent focus on the rural as romantic, magical or uncannily alien, there is also a long-established history of dramatic engagement with the pragmatic and political reality of the rural. In the context of British theatre this reaches back to the origins of British drama in the medieval mystery plays of the Corpus Christi cycles where, before the performance of the Annunciation to the shepherds, the actors playing those characters reminded their spectators of the practicalities of working life in the countryside. Some five hundred or so years before Butterworth's play attracted full houses and fulsome reviews at the Royal Court, the shepherds of the Towneley *Second Shepherds' Play* complained to their audience of the realities of rural life: livestock disease, physical hardship, enclosure and unhappy marriages which – they made clear – existed just as much in the country as in the city. Their experience of the rural is far from the idealised version of country life that the word might first summon to our imaginations:

But we sely husbands
That walks on the moor,
In faith we are nearhands
Out of the door.
No wonder, as it stands,
If we be poor,
For the tilth of our lands
Lies fallow as the floor,
As ye ken.
We are so hammed,
Fortaxed, and rammed,
We are made hand-tamed
With these gentlery-men. (Towneley *Second Shepherds' Play* in *Norton Anthology of English Literature*, 8th edn, vol. 1, 2005, p. 409)

'We are so hamstrung, /Overtaxed and beaten down', they claim. Writing about the pastoral ecology of the play and its companion, the Towneley *First Shepherds' Play*, Lisa J. Kiser identifies the major cause of the shepherds' suffering as being the system of enclosure which affected the lives of rural peasants during the period 1440–1450, by turning them from tenant farmers into wage labourers. As a result their 'identity with the land' was lost (2009, p. 338). That relationship with 'the land', embodied both by the shepherds in the *Second Shepherds' Play* and by Rooster and Davey in their very different ways in Butterworth's *Jerusalem*, is at the heart of this book, a key aim of which is to examine some of the different ways in which theatre has performed the rural from medieval to contemporary times.

It is worth noting that Kiser here seems to be invoking the sense of an earlier, better rural, capable of being lost, the turn towards enclosed pasture from shared commons 'destroy[ing] the cohesion of the medieval rural communities' (p. 338, citing Hilton, 1975, p. 168). The singing of Blake's poem as a hymn at the start of *Jerusalem* suggests, too, that there just might be a green and pleasant – and powerful – land, embodied by Rooster, which is similarly threatened by the bureaucracy of Kennet and Avon Council. Both Kiser and Butterworth point towards a rural ideal that is apparently always just disappearing, just out of reach. This is a key theme of 'Performing the rural', where I argue that in performances from the early modern period onwards, the rural often stands for a particular kind of 'otherness', to be visited and returned from, perhaps transformed.

Viewing the rural

One reason for that repeated turn to the 'lost' rural might of course be that the rural on stage is most often seen from the perspective of the city, where theatre and its associated buildings have historically and conventionally been situated. Claire Cochrane makes the case that an 'unexamined prejudice has driven much British theatre history to skew the record towards the assumption that everything important in British theatre happened in London' (2011, p. 3); I would argue further that theatre scholarship is often city-focused, whatever the nation being considered. In the *Cambridge Introduction to Theatre Studies*, for example, Christopher Balme states that 'a theatre building is part of the cognitive cartography of a town or city. Thus, a place of performance is determined by its integration into the wider referential system of the urban environment' (2008, p. 58). Balme's claims would be right for the majority of the plays and theatre spaces I've mentioned so far. Butterworth's play began life on the main stage of the Royal Court in London's Sloane Square (some fifty years after Wesker's *Roots* was staged there), next to Sloane Square underground station and just across from Peter Jones' department store, before travelling to Broadway and back to the Apollo Theatre on Shaftesbury Avenue in London's West End, where it was close by the Lyric, Gielgud and Queen's theatres and no more than a few minutes' walk from the neon lights and noise of Piccadilly Circus, not to mention the Houses of Parliament and Buckingham Palace.

Similarly, while theatre scholarship has often neglected the role of the spectator, what work *has* been done on audiences has focused on urban contexts, with little attention paid to rural audiences. Arguments about both the writer and the performance location of the Towneley pageant cycle mean that we cannot be totally sure where that play would have been performed. But perhaps the pragmatic reality of the *First* and *Second Shepherds' Plays* reflects the likelihood that the audiences for that mystery cycle – thought to be located in the then small West Yorkshire town of Wakefield in the mid-to-late fifteenth century – had a much closer relationship to the reality of rural life and work than might the citizens of York, an already substantial medieval city. The final section of this book thus considers the rural as a site of performance. By looking at theatre sited *in* the rural as well as *about* the rural, I aim to identify key questions about the relationship between place, audience and performance. How do theatre–audience relationships change when theatre comes to the audience, and to the place in the rural landscape where the audience is already 'at home'? More widely, given the increasing emphasis in social and political geography on rural, local communities as representing places of belonging and of shared knowledge which complicate and resist the apparent threat of globalisation, how might theatre of and in the rural help to build and complicate our 'sense of place and what constitutes it', in Paul Kingsnorth's terms (2008, p. 106)?

Defining the rural

> we have this beautiful earth. Very efficient, flat land, plough right up to edge, no waste. [...] We now among many illustrious landowners, Esso, Gallagher, Imperial Tobacco, Equitable Life, all love this excellent earth. How beautiful English countryside. [...] Now I find teashop, warm fire, old countryman to tell tales. (Caryl Churchill, *Fen*, 1990, p. 147)

The Japanese businessman whose voice frames the action in Caryl Churchill's play *Fen* (University of Essex Theatre,

Colchester, 1983) highlights two very different, but perhaps equally commodified views of the 'beautiful English countryside': as an economic resource for exploitation, and as a site for old countrymen to tell tourists tales. I will return to Churchill's play in more detail later; here her play's beginning helps to highlight the varied understandings of the rural that this section seeks to address.

In *Only Connect*, a report written for the UK's National Rural Touring Forum in 2004, François Matarasso argues that it is difficult to say what we mean by rural 'because non-urban Britain is so varied':

> It can mean the smoking pyres of healthy cattle [in the cattle culls precipitated by the foot and mouth disease outbreak of 2001], or the vegetable factories staffed by illegal workers under the gangmaster's thumb. It can mean wind farms and barn conversions, foxhunting and holiday cottages, isolated pensioners or old-fashioned village schools. Pick your own. (2004, p. 22)

Addressing a more global perspective, Keith Halfacree identifies a similarly varied range of conceptions, arguing that '"rural" can conjure up a huge range of spatial imaginaries. A list of these could include: countryside, wilderness, outback, periphery, farm belt, village, hamlet, bush, peasant society, pastoral, garden, unincorporated territory, open space' (2006, p. 45). And while this initial discussion of definitions focuses on the UK – and on what might perhaps be seen as a kind of *ur*-rural represented by the English pastoral idyll — my hope is that the issues addressed here and throughout the remainder of this volume will raise questions that resonate in other contexts wherever divisions between urban and rural landscapes and communities exist. For the rural is a key founding idea in other nations too: Stephen Wilmer highlights the role of the annual Chautauqua gatherings across the United States in the late nineteenth and early twentieth centuries in which national touring organisations sent out packages of plays, speeches and other amusements to small towns and villages that 'emphasised rural rather than urban values as the distinctive virtues of the nation', 'helping to solidify the notion that America was homogenous and rural' (2002, p. 11).

What *is* clear across all these understandings of the rural, however (as shown by Matarasso's rapid slip from 'rural' to 'non-urban', 2004, p. 22), is that the rural is repeatedly defined in relationship with the urban. UK government statisticians, too, place the rural at one end of a continuum with the urban. The official *Rural-Urban Classification for England* consists of six rural and four urban settlement/context combinations, dividing the rural into rural town and fringe, rural village, rural hamlet and isolated dwellings, each of which can also be additionally defined as being in a sparse setting (DEFRA, 2013); the Scottish government offers a choice of two-, three-, six- or eight-fold urban–rural classifications depending on the user's need (2014). Wales and Northern Ireland also highlight service provision and access as key, pointing out that definition depends on purpose:

which particular 'rural issues' are we trying to capture and what do we intend to use the classification for? If we are particularly interested in access to services issues, for example, we would use a different measure to one that is used to determine planning applications. (Welsh Statistical Directorate, 2008, p. 5)

Some figures may help clarify the relationship between the rural and urban: in England in 2011, 9.3 million people lived in *rural areas* (17.6 per cent of the population) – that is, in smaller towns (less than 10,000 people), villages, hamlets or isolated dwellings – but those rural areas made up 85 per cent of the land area (DEFRA, 2013). In addition to this statistically oriented focus, however, Lidia Varbanova's discussion of the diverse connotations of the term 'rural communities' in different countries across Europe adds an important affective dimension that is central to the argument within this book. Noting increasing difficulties in small and urbanised countries such as Belgium or the Netherlands in making a clear distinction between *urban* and *rural*, one of the definitions that she offers for rural place is where a population has 'a collective memory at a certain rural territory, and [...] a *sense of place*' (2009, p. 3, emphasis in original).

A rural sense of place

Varbanova's emphasis is also present in a number of other accounts of rural place. Matarasso argues that the rural is not just a question of geography or demography: 'Rural

Britain is a landscape of the mind, as well as a place where people live, work and play' (2004, p. 9). Marc Mormont similarly suggests that the rural is 'a category of thought' (1990, p. 40); in doing so he draws on an expanded geographical understanding of space and place that merits further exploration and explanation here. In their introduction to *Thinking Space*, Mike Crang and Nigel Thrift argue that geography has moved 'away from a sense of space as a practico-inert container of action towards space as a socially produced set of manifolds' (2000, p. 2). Following (and simplifying) Tim Cresswell's argument in *Place: A Short Introduction*, I take this definition of space as socially produced to mean that place is no longer seen as simply an area marked by coordinates on a map or – as in the definitions of the rural cited above – by the sparsity of population numbers or land-use statistics. Instead, it should be understood as 'constituted through reiterative social practice', through what is done in that place and, I would add, through what is said, written and performed about and within that place. As a result, Cresswell argues, 'Places are constructed by people doing things and in this sense are never "finished" but are constantly being performed' (2004, p. 37). As Halfacree points out, '*there is not one* [rural] *but there are many*' (citing Murdoch and Pratt, 1993, p. 425, emphasis added), although an understanding of rural place as produced through social enactment and representation is 'likely to contrast an imagined rural geography of landscape aesthetics and "community" with that of other spaces, notably the city/urban and the suburb' (2006, p. 47).

13

In an attempt to more fully understand the terms on which ideas of rural space are constructed and represented, Halfacree draws on Lefebvre's triadic model of social spaces, set out in his *The Production of Space* (1974, first published in English, 1991). Re-working Lefebvre's conceptual triad of space as perceived, conceived and lived, Halfacree identifies a three-fold architecture of rural space:

- *Perceived space*, or what Halfacree terms 'distinctive spatial practices', linked to either production or consumption (2006, p. 51). Historically, rural localities have been inscribed through the predominance of particular agricultural practices of food production, but also through agricultural cultural practices such as harvest festivals and other village celebrations.
- *Conceived space*, or what Halfacree terms 'formal representations of the rural', such as those expressed by business or commercial interests or politicians, which refer to the ways in which the rural is framed within capitalist processes of production and exchange (p. 54). The argument of this book is that theatre's representations of the rural can also operate as conceived space, performing key cultural work in establishing and reinforcing understandings of rural lives and experience for its audiences.
- *Lived space*, or what Halfacree terms the 'everyday lives of the rural', incorporating both 'individual and social elements ("culture") in their cognitive interpretation and negotiation' of rural life, and which are 'inevitably incoherent and fractured' (p. 51). I take this to mean

the individual, lived experience of the place of the rural which will be different according to the particular lives of each person, whether a contract farmworker from Poland working in Lincolnshire, a commuter escaping from the city for a more peaceful way of life, a B&B owner on the edges of a National Park or a teenager bussing daily from village to school.

All these elements interact at any given moment, so that the place of the rural always holds within it the different aspects of perceived, conceived and lived space that overlap with one another. And each of the elements is subject to change and development as the material practices of the rural change, with, in the UK context for example, a decline in agriculture and a rise in the importance of tourism to some areas of the rural economy.

However, in the context of this book, I want to suggest that what Halfacree calls the formal representations of the rural might be expanded beyond the range of policy documents to include the ways in which rural themes and lives are represented in and by theatre and performance. This is important because as Hamilton and Scullion (2004) suggest, the rural is too often categorised from an outside perspective as 'a romanticised space, a magical and uncanny space'. Theatre has contributed to that categorisation, as the following discussion of plays that put rural place onto the stages of our cities shows. In the history of the rural, the dominance of certain representations of the rural — where the perceiving is being done largely by outsiders located in the thought categories of the urban – repeatedly outweighs the lived reality of those who live and work within rural localities. Too often, as a rural interviewee in Michael Simmons' *Landscapes of Poverty* points out, 'There is no comprehension nationally of the rural perspective. Poverty in an age of affluence is being unable to write and have others write about you' (1997, p. 157). Lacking that rural perspective, idealised versions of the rural can obscure real-life rural conditions that urgently need addressing in social, political and economic terms, not least the poverty – both cultural and financial – that Simmons identifies. For example, while in the 1990s the English Countryside Commission was arguing for the importance of investment for 'keeping the countryside beautiful', research for the Rural Development Commission suggested that such 'beauty' obscured a disturbing reality. In nine out of the twelve areas studied for its *Lifestyles in Rural England* report, 20 per cent or more of rural households were living in or close to poverty (Cloke, Milbourne and Thomas, 1994).

However, the Countryside Commission's idealised view remains culturally dominant, not least because, as Williams recognised in *The Country and the City*, older ideas of the rural still persist even in an increasingly urban and industrial land:

> So much of the past of the country, its feelings and its literature, was involved with rural experience [...] that there is almost an inverse proportion, in the twentieth century, between the

relative importance of the working rural economy and the cultural importance of rural ideas. (1973, p. 248)

Part of the persistence of these ideas and experiences comes from the images and understandings created and reinforced through literature's long engagement with the concepts of, and relationship between, the city and the country which *The Country and the City* tracks from the seventeenth century onwards. From the pastoral poetry of the Renaissance to the novels of Jane Austen in which the country is 'weather or a place for a walk', or those of George Eliot who, Williams argues, restores the real inhabitants of rural England to their places but 'does not get much further than restoring them *as a landscape*' (1973, pp. 166, 168, emphasis in original), Williams identifies a sense of the rural as intimately connected to looking back to a pictorial and perhaps static past: 'the common image of the country is now an image of the past, and the common image of the city an image of the future' (p. 297). And while the book is largely focused on literary engagements with the English rural, the themes that emerge from his book are echoed in other national contexts. Edward Casey's *Getting Back into Place* (2009), which ranges across the globe in drawing examples of embodied place, operates between binaries of built places and wilderness spaces, with the latter increasingly viewed from the safe confines of the former. The lived and worked reality of the rural landscape is missing from these constructions of place, situated beyond the range of the viewer's or reader's experience.

Rural nostalgias

Running through the engagements with the country or wilderness in both these works by Williams and Casey is an undercurrent of nostalgia, perhaps implicit in Williams' sense of the country always being imaginatively located in the past. Despite recent attempts to reclaim nostalgia's power for the radical left, such as in Alastair Bonnett's *Left in the Past: Radicalism and the Politics of Nostalgia* (2010), the danger of nostalgia is indeed a real one, as Hamilton and Scullion (2004, p. 20) identify. Arguing the need for Irish theatre to embrace the profound changes that have affected that country in recent decades, Declan Hughes writes:

> Despite the fact that the overwhelming movements and changes in Irish society in the last thirty years have been urban, global, technological; that in every other area, we divest ourselves of the past like the good little I.T. loving global capitalists we're becoming; culturally we persist in defining ourselves by the ethnic, the pastoral (and that qualified form, the tragic pastoral). [...] I could live a long and happy life without seeing another play set in a Connemara kitchen, or a country pub. (2009, pp. 12–13)

Hughes here recognises – as does Williams – the power of culture to trap us in particular mindsets, suggesting that theatrical representations can act just as powerfully as policy makers' or governments' representations of space, in

Lefebvre's terms, to frame and shape our understanding of the rural, even if these representations are ostensibly positive ones. And these representations can have real-world effects, as Fintan O'Toole argues in his essay 'Going West: The Country Versus the City in Irish Writing' (1985). Here he suggests that the false opposition of the country and the city created by the dominance of the rural over the urban in Irish culture and writing 'has been vital to the maintenance of a conservative political culture in [Ireland]' (p. 111).

In 'Conceptualizing Rurality', Philip Cloke suggests,

> If at some point in the past some 'real' form of rurality was responsible for cultural mappings of rurality, it may now be the case that cultural mappings precede and direct the recognition of rural space, presenting us with some kind of virtual rurality. (2006, p. 22)

But it is important to understand that those cultural mappings are not necessarily fixed and innate. If, as Cresswell argues, place is socially constructed, always being performed, 'given that human forces made a place then human forces can equally importantly undo it' (2004, p. 30). Just as Jen Harvie argues in *Staging the UK*, that if national identities are creatively imagined, that means they are dynamic, and if they are dynamic, they can be changed (2005, p. 3), so I suggest here that these cultural mappings of the rural are also potentially dynamic and subject to change. Theatre, then, could have a key role to play in both producing and potentially changing understandings of the rural, challenging dominant views of the relationships between urban and rural which can affect the political, social and cultural lives of the nation. It is with this in mind that I now turn to look at the ways in which the rural has been represented and performed on stage from the early modern period to the present.

Performing the rural

> Plays about peasant life struggle against two big disadvantages. The first is a lowering of expectations on the playwright's part: a refusal to believe that the characters are capable of complex emotion. [...] But if playwrights are slow to take peasant life seriously, the public is slower still. (Eyre and Wright, *Changing Stages*, 2002, pp. 71–2)

Although the medieval shepherds of the Towneley *Second Shepherds' Play* may have shared with their audience an understanding of the reality of rural life as 'hammed, foretaxed, and rammed', more often the theatre written for and performed in the theatres of our cities has tended to use the rural to carry that freight of 'peace, innocence and simple virtue' identified by Williams in *The Country and the City*. The rural is rarely taken 'seriously', in Eyre's and Wright's terms. Adrienne Scullion's definition of pastoral in *The Oxford Encyclopedia of Theatre and Performance* (2010) as 'a form of drama evolved from poetry – particularly the idyll, eclogue or bucolic – which idealises nature and the rural life' underlines that conceptualisation. Scullion here emphasises the doubled, and divided, relationship between city and country that Williams so clearly identifies:

> Ostensibly the pastoral tells stories of shepherds but at root the form problematizes social relationships and ideas of modernization: the purity and simplicity of shepherd life is contrasted with the corruption and artificiality of the court, the town, or the city. (Scullion, 2010)

At the outset of what Scullion describes as 'perhaps the best known pastoral play', Shakespeare's *As You Like It* (c.1599), Charles, Duke Frederick's wrestler, gossips to Oliver about the exiled Duke Senior's life in the greenwoods in terms that are a pre-echo of *Jerusalem*'s own invocation of 'Woden. Jack of Green. [...] Brutus of Albion' and the 'green plains of England':

> They say he is already in the forest of Arden, and a many merry men with him; and there they live like the old Robin Hood of England: they say many young gentlemen flock to him every day, and fleet the time carelessly, as they did in the golden world. (Act 1, Sc. 1, 109–13)

The golden world of the forest described by Charles of course enables a series of transformations in the course of the play. It is the place where Rosalind disguises herself as the male youth Ganymede and woos Orlando on her own terms, and where the usurper Duke Frederick, coming to 'the skirts of this wild wood' in order to put his brother Duke Senior to the sword, is 'converted/ both from his enterprise and from the world' (Act 5, Sc. 4, 157–60). Oliver, too, is changed by his experiences in the forest: ''Twas I; but 'tis not I: I do not shame/ To tell you what I was, since my conversion/ So sweetly tastes, being the thing I am' (Act 4, Sc. 3, 138–40). Thus the wood, and the wider pastoral, is seen as a productive space in which 'positive' transformation occurs, resolving the hierarchical divisions and the overthrowing of 'natural' order that marks the beginning of Shakespeare's play.

But as Jane Kingsley-Smith's discussion in *Shakespeare's Drama of Exile* makes clear, such transformation is often focused on a return from the rural:

> Exile is often the means by which courtiers and shepherds meet in a bucolic landscape [...] the exile enters a pastoral landscape where shepherds offer succour and a new way of life [...] the pastoral sojourn ends with the reconciliation of family members and/or former enemies, often preceding a betrothal. At this point the exiles are enabled to return to society. (2003, pp. 106–7)

Such a definition, with its 'happy' conclusion in a return to 'society' that equates in meaning to the court or city space, itself can be seen to reproduce the kinds of value systems that I have already questioned in the earlier sections of this book. Kingsley-Smith highlights a recognisable pattern that we can identify in the pastoral sojourn of the Duke's Court and of Rosalind and Celia in Shakespeare's *As You Like It*, or the supernatural forest of *A Midsummer Night's Dream*. It's also present in more complicated ways in what Julie Sanders calls the 'politicised forest plays' of the 1640s, such as Richard Brome's *A Jovial Crew* (1641–2) and James Shirley's *The Sisters* (1642), which, she argues, 're-engage the by now familiar dramaturgic structure of an escape to the greenwoods and the formation of an alternative community there' (Sanders, 2014, p. 126). Such stories perhaps foreshadow the activities of the Levellers and Diggers of the English Civil War, who, as Caryl Churchill explores in her play *Light Shining in Buckinghamshire* (1976, Traverse Theatre, Edinburgh), began to dig up, manure and sow corn upon George Hill in Surrey, claiming in *The True Leveller's Standard Advanced* 'that England is not a free people till the poor that have no land have a free allowance to dig and labour the commons' (1985, p. 219). But the Diggers' rebellion was crushed by the military; similarly, in the drama of the early modern period, those alternative communities are usually only temporary, the plot resolved through a reintegration into society. Writing of Shakespeare's comedies in his *Anatomy of Criticism*, Northrop Frye identifies what he calls the 'drama of the green world', its plot being assimilated to the ritual theme of the triumph of life and love over the waste land: 'the action of the comedy begins in a world represented as a normal world, moves into the green world, goes into a metamorphosis there in which the comic resolution is achieved, and returns to the normal world' (1957, p. 182). Here the 'normal' is contrasted with the magical and other space of the green world.

Sanders' gesture towards politicisation does, however, suggest a more complicated version of the rural, beyond the enchanted forest of *A Midsummer Night's Dream* or *As You Like It*, even in early modern theatre. Indeed, John Kerrigan suggests in his discussion of the aged Gloucestershire Justices Shallow and Silence who appear in *Henry IV Part 2* as hosts to young Prince Hal's comic and cowardly companion, Falstaff, as he journeys across the kingdom seeking recruits for battle, that 'Gloucestershire was no backwater', instead being positioned as 'a cross-roads between North and West with thriving ports and affluent hinterland' (1990, p. 27). Nor, Kerrigan argues, should what he terms 'the post-Restoration tendency of theatre to find rural life inane obscure the importance of Shallow's farm': the context of grain shortages across the country by 1597 would mean that the farm, 'far from being a bucolic retreat, would be a venture of immediate interest' (pp. 27–8). The 'distinctive spatial practices' of the rural had a key part to play in the functioning economy of early modern England, yet the representation of the rural in the play is surely solely a humorous one. The Justices and their roll of potential recruits for the battle – Moldy, Shadow, Wart, Feeble and Bullcalf – are positioned as a comic interlude in the play, where Falstaff's and Bardolph's London wit is seen to skewer the failings of both the recruits and their hosts.

Whatever their politics, however, it is important to remember that most of these plays were first written for city stages, thus playing a key part in the development of the rural as a conceived space, in Lefebvre's terms. Their audiences, as Kerrigan suggests, might have a less bucolic, more commercial, understanding of the countryside, but the rural was still an area for exploitation, whether in terms of wheat and rye or – as in the darkly comic scenes of the mustering of men by Falstaff – of men to serve in the King's wars. As a place of exile or as comedy, the rural was different, other, something to be looked at: a tendency which perhaps reached its nadir in the pictorial stagings of the late nineteenth and early twentieth centuries when, as David Bevington highlights in his description of Oscar Asche's production of *As You Like It* at His Majesty's Theatre in 1907, two thousand pots of ferns and cartloads of leaves were imported weekly to create the aura of a real forest (2012, p. 33).

This brief discussion of the early modern theatre's engagement with the rural, then, raises a number of different possible representations or imaginings of the rural which have continued to resonate across the centuries that followed: the rural as a place of exile as for Duke Senior in *As You Like It*; the rural as a transformational, or liminal space as for Rosalind in the same play; the rural as something alien or other, whether humorously as in *Henry IV*

Part 2 or more dangerously so; the rural as representative
of national identity, perhaps idealised as 'the golden world'
of old Robin Hood of England described by Charles the
wrestler in *As You Like It*. In what follows, I briefly trace
those themes through a discussion of twentieth and twenty-
first-century plays and performances which similarly seem
to place the rural at a distance from their contemporary
audiences, arguing that the rural 'landscape of the mind',
in Matarasso's words, is rarely a mutually understood or
represented one. Extended textual analysis of these plays is
already widely available; here I concentrate on identifying
the ways in which the themes already identified – of exile
and transformation, of nostalgia and of rural othering –
persist and linger as cultural mappings of the rural, across
the decades and in both UK and international contexts.

Rural freedoms, rural exiles

> It is an Englishman's duty at the first scent of
> May to make the turf his floor, his roof the arc-
> ing firmament. [...] This is a time for revelry.
> [...] To be free from constraint. (Butterworth,
> *Jerusalem*, pp. 51–2)

The words of the wandering Professor in Butterworth's
play express an enthusiasm for the rural and rural customs
that suggests a place of freedom and unrestraint, even if the
lyricism of his claims is soon undercut by the laughter of
Rooster's young companions. Rooster's forest clearing does

seem to offer a place of freedom to both the Professor and the youth of the nearby village, as well as to the spectators in the audience. And as we have seen, from the theatre of the early modern period onwards, the forest or the countryside has repeatedly offered a space to be different, a depiction of the rural that Rabey characterises in his discussion of Butterworth's earlier theatre as 'the possible refuge of the idiosyncratic outsider' (2015, p. 109). From the 'jovial crew' of Brome's play of the same title, who leave their country houses to travel with the beggars and vagabonds of the rural roads, to Arnold Wesker's naïve young couple Dave and Ada Simmonds in his 1960 play *I'm Talking about Jerusalem*, who move to Norfolk on a surge of postwar optimism in search of a different mode of living, the rural seems to offer an alternative space in which a different kind of life can be lived. As Dave declares to the removal men in Wesker's play, 'us poor city sods' who have brought their belongings to their new country home:

> [My family] will share in my work and I shall share in their lives. I don't want to be married to strangers. I've seen the city make strangers of husbands and wives, but not me, not me and my wife.
> (*The Wesker Trilogy*, 1964, p. 165)

But where Northrop Frye's description of 'green world' dramas as transformative holds true for *As You Like It*, *A Midsummer Night's Dream* and Brome's *A Jovial Crew*, Wesker's twentieth-century version of the move from city to rural and back again is presented in rather more depressing terms. Located entirely in the setting of the Norfolk house to which the Simmonds move at the beginning of Act 1 and leave at the end of Act 3, returning to London, the play undermines the main characters' initial optimism that the country might offer a different way of living. Like Shakespeare's protagonists, Dave and Ada return from the country at the end of the play, but here there has been no transformation except that of failure, their experiment in alternative living having petered out. While Steve Waters sees Butterworth's *Jerusalem* as somehow pausing temporality in 'a wonderfully halting tempo of action' in *The Secret Life of Plays* (2010, p. 91), Dave and Ada soon discover that their own hoped-for Jerusalem is governed by the same temporal pressures as their previous lives in the city. Dave's new employer, the Colonel, arrives as they unpack and insists on an early beginning to work. 'We're still rushing', says Dave (p. 170), and indeed they never manage to escape the temporality of the outside world, a point emphasised by the radio that plays over the start of the final scene, announcing the 1959 election results which 'ensure the return to power in the House of Commons of the Conservative Party for a third time in succession since the end of the war' (p. 208). The couple's efforts to build their own Jerusalem fail and they return to the city, their country house now just a holiday home. The 'green world', which initially seemed to offer freedom, or the possibility of a socialist ideal, thus remains resolutely untransformative. Perhaps this is because, as Ada's mother Sarah Kahn identifies early in the play, this rural 'Jerusalem' has always just been an ivory tower for the couple, rather than a real place: it is conceived space, in Lefebvre's and Halfacree's terms, rather than the understood, everyday reality of the negotiation and interpretation of rural life.

Where Dave and Ada – and perhaps the audiences of Wesker's play – persist in seeing the rural in idealised terms of freedom and transformation despite the play's undermining of such ideals, Edward Bond's 1974 *Bingo: Scenes of Money and Death* (Northcott Theatre, Exeter) presents an interestingly different take on the green world dramas of transformation considered here. In it Bond shows us his character, Shakespeare, making a journey from London, the city of his successful career in theatre, back to his home in rural Warwickshire. The terms of the green world journey are here reversed, the 'normal' perhaps being the rural rather than the urban: and although in some ways transformed through his playwriting career (Ben Jonson turns up to drink with Shakespeare in the Golden Cross Inn in Scene Four of the play), Bond's Shakespeare is shown as caught up in the economics and politics – the scenes of money and death – that affect the rural just as much as the urban, leading to his suicide in the final scene of the play. A local landowner, 'Combe, schemes to get richer by enclosing the fields around Stratford. A revolutionary Puritan movement, a little like the historical Diggers, arises briefly in reaction against the enclosures. Agricultural labourers carry out small acts of sabotage' (Mangan, 1998, p. 34). Here Bond shows us the writer responsible for developing the very pattern of green world drama in Frye's terms as encountering a very different rural, one in which the spatial practices of production and consumption are being actively contested and changed. And Bond's Shakespeare, poet of the green world, is shown as implicated in these changes.

Bond's introduction to his play makes his point explicit, rejecting the idea of the rural as any more free, or transformative, than any other space:

> We live in a closed society where you need money to live. You earn it, borrow it, or steal it. Criminals, and hermits or drop-outs, depend on others who earn money – there's no greenwood to escape into any more, it's been cut down. (1999, pp. 6–7)

Despite Jonson's question, 'Down here for the peace and quiet? Find inspiration – look for it anyway' (p. 44), the rural is here shown as just as cruel, just as enmeshed in the structures of capital and production, as the city. Bond's play both stands out as different, yet still – in his understanding that the greenwood has 'been cut down' – seems to look back, just as the Towneley shepherds did, to a better rural time when the possibility of rural freedom was perhaps still a reality. The unease and disillusionment with the nostalgic idea of the rural present in very different ways in Wesker's and Bond's plays is also reflected in those plays which more obviously situate the rural as other and different, to which I now turn.

Rural as other: from *Roots* to Rudkin and beyond

I'm Talking about Jerusalem is the third, least-often performed play in the trilogy of plays by Wesker that also
includes *Chicken Soup with Barley* (1958), set in London's
East End, and 1959's *Roots*, both also performed at the
Belgrade Theatre Coventry before transferring to London's
Royal Court. It's this central part of the trilogy that I want
to consider now as an example of a play in which, I'd argue,
the rural is constructed as other, even though the focus
is ostensibly on those who live and work there. In *Roots*,
Wesker switches perspective from that of the London Kahn
family to the lives of the Norfolk Bryants, framed through
the visit of Beatie Bryant home from her job as a waitress in
London and keenly anticipating the visit of her boyfriend,
Ronnie Kahn, to meet her family for the first time. Often
situated as part of the movement towards 'kitchen sink'
drama which took theatre out of the drawing rooms of Noel
Coward and Terence Rattigan and into the real lives of the
working classes, *Roots* differs in one important respect:
where the kitchen of John Osborne's 1956 *Look Back in
Anger* was situated in a Midlands city and Shelagh Delaney's
1958 *A Taste of Honey* was set in a shabby flat in Salford,
Wesker's characters were located in a rural setting, initially
in 'a rather ramshackle house in Norfolk where there is no
water laid on, nor electricity, nor gas. Everything rambles
and the furniture is cheap and old'. Wesker's stage description thus foreshadows the complaints of the Kahns in his
final play: 'No roads, no electricity, no running water, no
proper lavatory. It's the Middle Ages' (1964, p. 160). But

where *I'm Talking about Jerusalem* never attempts to show its audiences the rural from the perspective of those who live within it, *Roots'* kitchen sink reality perhaps initially suggests a changed point of view. Wesker's long stage direction in Act One stresses the importance for the director of 'organising' the silences in the play: 'the silences are important – as important as the way they speak, *if we are to know them*' (1964, p. 92, emphasis added). But our knowing of these characters, I want to argue here, is compromised from the outset by the terms of the rest of that stage direction, which suggests an othering of rural lives, marking them as alien from the early audiences of the play at the Belgrade, Coventry or London's Royal Court, to which the play soon transferred:

> They continue in a routine rural manner. The day comes,
> one sleeps at night, there is always the winter, the spring,
> the autumn, and the summer – little amazes them.

The apparent realism of the rural representation in fact masks a utilisation of the countryside as a place of ignorance: the 'rural manner' the 'other' to urban enlightenment. The kitchen sink realism may have moved on from the post-Restoration representation of the stupid country people in plays such as William Wycherley's *The Country Wife* (1675, Theatre Royal Drury Lane) that Kerrigan gestures towards in his essay '*Henry IV* and the Death of Old Double', but rural lives are still represented as inane and different.

Such an understanding is perhaps complicated by the audience's likely identification with the figure of Beatie, the returner from the city who has experienced both ways of living and brings with her into the houses of her Norfolk family a magpie collection of Ronnie's ideas and stances. Thus while Beatie – slipping back into Norfolk dialect – is of the rural, her stance is critical and increasingly distanced from the rural lives and perceptions she once shared. She is a liminal figure, belonging neither in the country nor in London, able at different moments in the play to critique both Ronnie's idealised sense of her family 'living in mystic communion with nature. Living in mystic bloody communication with nature (indeed)' (Wesker, 1964, *Roots*, p. 147), and what she increasingly understands as her family's narrow conception of life:

> [Y]ou live in the country but you got no – no – no majesty. You spend your time among green fields [...] and you breathe fresh air and you got no majesty. Your mind's cluttered up with nothing and you shut out the world. (p. 127)

Given the sympathies with Beatie that the play cultivates, Wesker's representation of the Norfolk Bryants is surely a critical one. As Christopher Innes suggests, 'the isolated Norfolk cottages are a microcosm for regressive attitudes' and 'anti-cultural proletarianism is presented as "*lumpen-proletariat*" brutishness' (1992, p. 115). Despite the country setting, Wesker and his character Beatie identify that the characters have no place in the world, no roots:

> It's not only the corn that need strong roots, you know, it's us too. But what've we got? Go on, tell me, what've we got? We don't know where we push up from and we don't bother neither. (1964, p. 146)

Innes argues for the 'comparative irrelevance of the Norfolk background' to the play (1992, p. 116), and certainly Wesker's note on pronunciation at the start of the published text suggests that the specifics of Norfolk location matter only for dialect, not for any greater understanding of what Halfacree terms the 'everyday lives of the rural' (2006, p. 51) as experienced by those who live and work in the East Anglian agricultural countryside. Beatie's triumphant final speech as, facing the disappointment of Ronnie's failure to arrive, she begins to find her own voice – 'God in heaven, *Ronnie*! It does work, it's happening to me, I can feel it's happened, I'm beginning, on my own two feet – I'm beginning ...' – is in performance accompanied by

> [t]he murmur of the family sitting down to eat [which] grows as BEATIE's last cry is heard. Whatever she will do they will continue to live as before. (p. 148)

The country and the people who live and work within it are thus a mere backdrop to Beatie's journey, reduced almost to dumb animals in these closing moments of the play, devoid of the capacity to feel or to change. Raymond Williams' sense of the inhabitants of rural England 'as a landscape' in the nineteenth-century novels of George Eliot resonates in relation to Wesker too.

If the *lumpenproletariat* Norfolk Bryants represent a particular view of rural lives, 'stubborn, empty, wi' no tools for livin'' (1964, p. 145), the agricultural labourers of David Rudkin's *Afore Night Come* (Arts Theatre, London, 1962) represent a still darker imagining of the rural as other. Set against his characterisation of Butterworth's earlier engagements with the rural as 'the possible refuge of the idiosyncratic outsider', Rabey offers a contrasting perspective drawn from what he sees as echoes of Rudkin's work: one in which he argues that Butterworth perceives the rural as 'a possible location for prejudice, scapegoating and surprisingly vicious sacrificial reflexes and rituals' (2015, p. 109). This is an accurate description of Rudkin's play, restaged by Peter Hall as part of the RSC's Theatre of Cruelty season at the Aldwych in 1964, in which the action is set against the context of a Black Country orchard where six hundred boxes of pears destined for Doncaster have to be filled 'afore night come'. As the watching audience, we enter the orchard alongside two new employees, Larry and Jeff, the former a student from Birmingham – or 'Brummagem', in the dialect of the fruit pickers. A third newcomer, Roche, an Irish tramp, subsequently appears and becomes the target of increasing hostility among the group. A series of repeated motifs, initially jokey – last year's students having their heads cut off because they left the straps on their buckets too long, students disappear-ing ('Oh, it'm utter, their disap-bloody-pearance' (1963, p. 89) – gradually darken in tone. Two of the regular work-ers, 'mad' Johnny Hobnails and Tiny, both born again Christians, claim to have been baptised 'in the Blood', and Johnny attempts, increasingly desperately, to persuade Larry to leave the orchard. However, it is Roche, not Larry, who becomes the sacrificial victim of what we come to real-ise is the orchard's regular, horrifying ritual, as a helicopter spraying pesticide 'screams down overhead':

> *Abnormal light. ROCHE bent back like a hoop, head front, face slashed. [...] ALBERT and JIM haul Jeff's arms down. Knife plunges. JEFF groans. GINGER hauls his wrists down twice more, knife with them each time, at breast, and heart. JEFF is moaning ... he has slashed on Roche's chest the form of a cross ... ROCHE falls, is still.* (Rudkin, 1963, pp. 132–3)

Roche's decapitated body is buried reverently, and Larry subsequently returns to the orchard, finding Jeff's knife and realising, as he is asked to return the next day, that his name has not been entered into the foreman's book; it becomes clear to both the character and the audience that had Roche not appeared Larry, as outsider, would have been the ritual victim. Discussing the play in his book *David Rudkin: Sacred Disobedience*, Rabey suggests that its originality lies in part in its 'location of drama's province and potential beyond the superficialities of the English domestic interior': '*Afore Night Come* depicts its own forms of repression, rhetoric and witticisms, but loads them with an irrational danger alien to most representations of the conventional bourgeois milieu'. He characterises the play as 'a portrait of an isolated community, beleaguered and vengeful, insistent on its own terms of definition' (Rabey, 1997, p. 20). But if the play itself creates a ritual, protective isolation against the perceived danger of outsiders, with Roche marked out as other both because of his use of language – 'got a poet in the orchard with us, now. Bloody Shakespeare' (p. 84) – and his ethnicity – 'well, well, well, if it ain't the playboy of the bleeding Western world' (p. 102) – for the audience at the Arts Theatre Club or the Aldwych, it is surely the rural itself that Rudkin's play constructs as other, and alien. The move from the English domestic interior to the rural exterior identified by Rabey is one of alienation and cruelty: as the audience enters the rural scene with the outsiders, Larry and Jeff, our initiation into the rural ritual is as reluctant as theirs. Jeff's hands are held by Ginger to slash Roche with the cross; his groans as he does so are surely ours, too.

A similar move is made in Michel Marc Bouchard's more recent *Tom à la ferme* (*Tom at the Farm*, 2011, Théâtre d'Aujourd'hui, Montreal). Tom's journey to attend the funeral of his unnamed lover takes him from the city to the countryside, to 'a dairy farm in rural Ontario'. Once at the farm, unable to tell the truth about his homosexual relationship, he is drawn into dysfunctional family relationships that become increasingly violent. Dragged 'tied by the wrists, on my belly for two kilometres', and later shown hanging upside down from a rope above a ditch filled with cow carcasses, Tom nevertheless becomes passionately immersed in the visceral life of the rural: 'Things are real around here. There's a dog that barks and you can hear it. [...] There's a calf that's born and there's blood' (2013, p. 66). Bouchard's preface to the play makes it clear that 'every day, gay youth are victims of aggression in school yards, at home, at work, on playing fields, in both urban and rural environments'. But the choice to make Tom's journey to revelation and violence one that moves from the city to the rural, and unleashes a kind of raw power there, suggests that in this play, too, 'the farm' functions as a particularly potent site for repression and violence. All these plays take us out of the city and into the country, but in each we as audience, in Coventry, London or Montreal, see the rural through other eyes, that mark it as different and strange.

The rural as the nation

Rabey suggests that the portrait of an isolated community created in *Afore Night Come* 'is in some ways closer to Irish dramatic images of cultural periphery, myth, crisis and continuity' (1997, p. 20) than to English ones. Here, however, I want to examine representations of the rural in Irish drama from a different perspective, arguing that it is perhaps most explicitly in Irish theatre that we are offered a different and potentially more positive understanding of the rural as representative of national identity.

In her 1995 'Place and Identity: A Sense of Place', Gillian Rose draws on Stephen Daniels' understanding, in his book *Fields of Vision: Landscape Imagery and National Identity in England and the United States*, of national identities as defined by 'legends and landscapes' (Daniels, 1993, p. 5) to suggest that historically, Ireland has imagined itself as a nation through rural representations, not least representations of the rural West of Ireland. To Irish nationalists at the beginning of the twentieth century, Rose argues, the West seemed to offer an explicit contrast with the pastoral English rural which has largely been the focus of this book so far:

> Because of what [Irish] nationalist writers saw as the closeness of the people of the West to this wild landscape, westerners came to embody all the virtues of Irishness. They were steadfast, dignified and strong, their relationship to the land a source of stability and calm determination. (1995, p. 91)

The West of Ireland, Rose argues, thus 'remains an important symbol of, and location for, Irishness' (p. 91). But while the painted landscapes considered by Daniels are pictorial, static and contained within the painting's frame, theatre's creation and peopling of such landscapes on the stage enables a more complicated view of the rural's relationship to national identity. I explore these ideas further here in relation to the Irish rural as staged in the work of two 'Irish' playwrights, writing at the beginning and end of the twenti-eth century, John Millington Synge and Martin McDonagh.

Shaun Richards highlights that the representation of rural Ireland was integral to the early work of the Abbey Theatre Dublin, itself in effect an Irish national theatre cre-ated through the union of the earlier Irish Literary Theatre and the Irish National Dramatic Company at the start of the twentieth century: 'it was this location "of pure, Catholic, native Ireland" which was the defining stage-set of the Abbey theatre between 1902 to 1908 when it "produced twice as many peasant plays as poetic plays"' (2006, pp. 247–8, citing Clarke, 1982, p. 1). Fintan O'Toole notes that the focus on rural life aimed to produce 'a political image of the countryside which helped to create a sense of social cohe-sion in a country that was trying to define itself over against England' (1985, p. 112). But by drawing on these idealised images, the founders of the Abbey Theatre can be criticised for neglecting the reality of rural life and the histories of poverty and famine that marked rural existence in the nine-teenth and early twentieth centuries: O'Toole goes on to argue that these Irish revival writers ignored the reality that rural Ireland was not a peasant paradise but a money econ-omy riven by class divisions (p. 113). Among these peasant plays was the controversial 1907 production of Synge's *The Playboy of the Western World*, in which the fleeing Christy Mahon turns up in a tavern in County Mayo, full of lurid tales of killing his father, and becomes a romantic hero to the town before his claims are undermined by the appear-ance of his wounded, but still living, parent. Attacked by

Irish nationalists for its representation of women and sexuality, the play famously prompted riots during its first run at the Abbey.

In 'Defining the rural' I argued that if, as Cloke suggests, 'cultural mappings precede and direct the recognition of rural space' (2006, p. 22), then theatre can play a key role in either reinforcing or – potentially – changing understandings of the rural. Thus, if the rural West somehow stands for, and in place of, the Irish nation, it is perhaps not surprising that such controversy was roused by the work of Synge in *Playboy* and again at the end of the twentieth century by McDonagh, whose Leenane and Aran Islands plays, starting with *The Beauty Queen of Leenane* (Town Hall Theatre, Galway and Royal Court, 1996) and finishing with *The Lieutenant of Insishmore* (RSC, The Other Place, 2001), represent the West as a place of almost cartoonish violence and madness. While the bloody violence of *Afore Night Come* is safely distanced from its London audience, the long tradition whereby the rural West stands for the Irish nation produces more complex and troubling effects.

Both playwrights draw on the tools of realism to delineate their rural settings, suggesting an authenticity of representation. Synge's play is set in what Nicolas Grene describes as a 'convincingly local locality' which stages 'not just a mapped reality of place but the mental landscape of a small community' through his use of family names and place names (1999, p. 98), while Richards highlights McDonagh's 'almost endless listing of products and programmes from Taytos [crisps] and Kimberly biscuits to *Star Wars* and

41

afternoon soap-operas' in his tales of rural Irish life (2006, pp. 249–50). But as Innes points out, 'the isolated Mayo village, to which the fleeing Christy comes [in *Playboy*] is not the green world of Arcadian Pastoral' (1992, p. 226). Instead in the work of both playwrights the audience encounters a world of violence and madness, infused with what Richards describes as 'the pervasive sense of bodily functions, sexual desire, blasphemy, and general degeneracy' (2006, p. 251). It is perhaps unsurprising, as Richards highlights, that they should have provoked such strong and remarkably similar reactions from contemporary critics.

These concerns become particularly problematic, Patrick Lonergan argues, because such work 'feeds into preconceptions about Irish ill discipline and primitivism' (2006, p. 312). The problem of these particular representations of the rural thus goes beyond a nostalgic yearning for a past before the rise and fall of the Irish Celtic Tiger economy in the early twenty-first century, and instead to the heart of the relationship between national identity and rural representation. Again I want to suggest here that looking back to Lefebvre and Halfacree, it is the way that the plays of Synge and McDonagh relate to the holding – and reinforcing – of such preconceptions by audiences situated *outside* the rural that is key to understanding this reception. Grene argues that:

> Irish drama is outward-directed, created as much
> to be viewed from outside as from inside Ireland.
> Even where the plays are produced wholly within

an Irish theatrical milieu, the otherness of Ireland as subject is so assumed by the playwrights as to create the effect of estranging exteriority. (1999, p. 3)

Even within Ireland, Grene suggests, 'on the whole Irish drama has continued to look to social margins for its setting [...]. It is thus typically other people that a largely middle-class urban audience watches in an Irish play' (p. 264). Grene's analysis again emphasises the ways in which the rural as other – even when standing in some way for the whole nation – is distanced from the spectators in the theatre auditorium, whether in Dublin or, as with McDonagh, in the National Theatre on London's Southbank or on New York's Broadway. Given my repeated stress on representation in this book, it is perhaps also important to note that those doing the representing here, Synge and McDonagh, are themselves both situated outside the places about which they write, with Synge educated and living in Dublin while McDonagh grew up in South London, only visiting Connemara on summer holidays with his extended Irish family. Lonergan suggests that it is precisely when McDonagh's tales of rural Ireland make that move out of Ireland that audiences throughout the world 'receive his plays in ways that reinforce negative thinking about Ireland' (2006, p. 316). But Lionel Pilkington's discussion of the first play in McDonagh's Leenane trilogy, *The Beauty Queen of Leenane*, highlights that Lonergan's Irish 'local' is itself divided, with the rural Ireland represented in McDonagh's plays abandoned both culturally and physically by his audience (2010, p. 71). Just as the Irish tramp Roche's 'otherness' in Rudkin's *Afore Night Come* leads the other fruit pickers to call him the 'playboy of the bleeding Western world', here the Irish rural is marked as different for the Irish metropolitan audiences: the site of performance and the site of representation enable a gap to open up between conceived space and lived space, in Lefebvre's terms, even when the represented place somehow holds within it the identity of a nation.

Rural stories, rural radicals

That gap between conceived space and lived space, between representations of the rural and the everyday lives of the rural, has marked each of the three categories of representation examined so far. Mike Pearson – a practitioner of site-specific performance to whose work I will return in the final section of this book – draws on the work of geographer Doreen Massey in ways that work to close that gap, and to highlight an understanding of place as produced: 'as that actively worked, that actively brought into being':

> what is special about place is not some romance of a pre-given collective identity or of the eternity of the hills. Rather what is special about place is precisely that throwntogetherness, the unavoidable challenge of negotiating a here and now (itself drawing on a history and geography of thens and theres); and a negotiation which

must take place within and between both human and nonhuman. (Massey, 2005, p. 140, cited in Pearson, 2010, pp. 108–9)

What Pearson and Massey remind us of here is that represented space – which we have repeatedly seen is too often nostalgic and romantic in relation to the rural focused on in this book, supposing an unchangedness of rural space as escape or other – is in fact a place made up of 'collections of [stories-so-far], articulations within the wider power-geometries of space' (Massey, 2005, p. 130). Paying attention to the particularity of rural place, and to the multiplicity of rural voices, fractured and incoherent though they may be, should thus be key to both the performance practice and the structures through which theatre approaches the stories and lives of rural places. If as Simmons' interviewee suggested, 'Poverty in an age of affluence is being unable to write and have others write about you' (1997, p. 157), it is important to enable rural voices to speak, and this is where theatre has a potentially key role to play in creating new understandings of the complexity and variation in the everyday lives of the rural. Indeed, Nell Leyshon, writer of a series of plays about rural life from 2001's *The Farm* onwards, makes clear the importance of doing so given the neglect of the rural in British national conversation:

Just after the war, there were 21 farms in the village. When I was living there as a child there were 14. Now there are one and a half, and it has

> become a dormitory village. It seems shocking
> that no one noticed. Everyone noticed the ship-
> yards going, everyone noticed the coal mines
> going. Nobody noticed what happened to farm-
> ing. ('Playwright who ploughs her own furrow',
> *Daily Telegraph*, 13 January 2007)

Creating a space for rural stories – and for the multiplicity of voices within rural environments – is thus the focus
of the final plays I examine in 'Performing the rural', in
which I place Leyshon's work alongside that of another,
long-established, woman playwright, Caryl Churchill.
Leyshon's work in *The Farm*, which was produced by Strode
Theatre Company and toured the South West before going
to Southwark Playhouse in 2002, was dedicated to 'the lost
farms of Central Somerset' and drew on her experiences
of growing up in a rural farming community there in its
delineation of a farming family struggling to keep going
when 'a pig costs sixty quid to raise and we get fifty-four
quid for it' (2002, p. 43). Churchill's earlier *Fen* (1983,
University of Essex Theatre, Colchester) also incorporated
the actual experiences and voices of rural inhabitants, as it
was developed through an extended workshop residency in
the Fens with Joint Stock theatre group, in which the company talked to as many local people as possible about their
lives. As Elaine Aston highlights, the young women in the
community are shown as having aspirations, represented
through the lyrics of the 'Girl's song', 'but ultimately their

dreams do not take them beyond the village which binds them to harsh work on the land, early marriages and child-rearing' (2001, p. 66): 'I want to be a nurse when I grow up/ And I want to have children and get married./ But I don't think I'll leave the village when I grow up' (Churchill, 1990, p. 157). Thus, in contrast to the green world dramas which always involve a journey and return, Leyshon and Churchill focus on the lives that belong to and remain in the rural, often trapped there by economic and social circumstances.

Indeed, these plays make explicit the impact of the globalisation and capitalism that produce those economic and social circumstances. Churchill's Japanese businessman references Esso and Imperial Tobacco as landowners, while Nell, one of the women farm workers in the play, asks, 'So who's boss? Who do you have a go at? Acton's was Ross, Ross is Imperial Foods, Imperial Foods is Imperial Tobacco, so where does that stop?' (1990, p. 181). This alienation from the land is also highlighted in Leyshon's play, where the farm's milk cattle have all been killed and the son and heir to the farm, Gavin, goes out to find a job in the supermarket, his father realising that 'People don't want what I can grow anymore':

> I'll tell you what people want. They want their
> potatoes in boxes, all washed, all the same size.
> [...] They want their meat cheap, never mind
> how it's raised, how it's killed. They want to eat

things their grandparents never knew existed,
and they don't want to wait till they're in season.
They know nothing about food. (Leyshon, 2002,
p. 41)

However, despite this sense of increasing separation from
the land, I argue that both plays offer a more nuanced view
of the rural, and of rural nostalgia, than we have encoun-
tered so far in this book. Churchill makes the past and the
present visible on the stage simultaneously: as the audience
enters, a 'boy from the last century, barefoot and in rags, is
alone in a field, in a fog, scaring crows' (1990, p. 147). Later
in the play the farmer, Tewson, has himself sold his land to
a city institution which claims that, 'with us, your grandson
will farm his grandfather's acres' (p. 162), and encounters a
ghost working in his field:

I been working in this field a hundred and fifty
years. There ain't twenty in this parish but what
hates you, bullhead. [...] I live in your house. I
watch television with you. I stand beside your
chair and watch the killings. I watch the food and
I watch what makes people laugh. My baby died
starving. (p. 163)

Through a series of scenes that interweave past and present
lives, Churchill reveals the dispiriting and violent reality of
living and working in the Fenland landscape, a landscape that
has, it seems, always been owned by others. The original stage

design by Annie Smart covered the entire surface of the playing space with soil, in which the (largely) women workers are seen harvesting potatoes, sorting onions and stone picking, but also carrying out their household chores: in a final dreamlike sequence which connects the voice of the murdered character Val with the ghosts which haunt the Fenland landscape, Shirley is seen 'ironing the field' (p. 189). Sheila Rabillard notes that as the play progressed, the dirt 'progressively dusted the costumes of the actors', 'connecting [the] human inhabitants of the fen to the source of their sustenance even though that relationship has been vitiated by capitalism' (2009, p. 92). The play thus seems to move towards a shared relationship with the land, what Rabillard describes as a 'human (and non-human) sharing in the world's resources' (p. 93).

Similarly, despite Leyshon's dedication of her play to the 'lost farms', *The Farm* ends with a focus on the now, and a lack of regret:

> I sat on the hill this morning, like all those times, and thought even if we lose the farm, we'll have been here. We'll have looked after it, you'll have done what you did. Made your mark. And I thought as I sat there that whatever happens, wherever we end up, I've never regretted any of this. That's all. That's all I wanted to say. (2002, p. 72)

With their focus on the actual lives of those who live and work in the rural environment, and the attempt to tell their stories from the perspectives of those inhabitants, both plays thus seem to play an important part in what Anna Harpin has more recently identified as a new ruralism and 'the resurgence of the local' in her 2011 article 'Land of Hope and Glory: Jez Butterworth's Tragic Landscapes'. Noting the 'recent theatrical return of the countryside to the city stages' in plays such as Butterworth's *Jerusalem*, Peter Gill's *The York Realist* (2001, Lowry Theatre), Martin Crimp's *The Country* (2000, Royal Court), Nell Leyshon's *Comfort Me with Apples* (2005, Hampstead Theatre), Richard Bean's *Harvest* (2005, Royal Court) and Butterworth's earlier *The Night Heron* (2002, Royal Court), Harpin argues that this renewed focus on the rural and local 'marks a coun-termove to the non-spaces and boundary-less homogeneity of global capital and its devastating environmental conse-quences' (2011, pp. 65, 66). It is in this context that Alistair Bonnett's work on re-reading nostalgia suggests the possi-bility for a radical space of resistance, when 'the aspiration to plough up the past and cover the world in shining new cities of tomorrow has lost its appeal. [...] So we turn away and back to things that remain worth fighting for and which sustain' (2010 p. 173).

At the conclusion of his article, 'Rural Space: Constructing a Three-fold Architecture', Halfacree also gestures towards a more radical claim for the potentiality of the rural. While noting that rural place has from some perspectives largely been 'effaced by the geographical devel-opment of late capitalism [...] leaving rural space only as a ghostly presence, experienced through folk memory, nostalgia, hearsay, etc.', he goes on to suggest that there is potential in producing different, radical versions of the rural:

> Thinking of the content of this 'radical' rural space, we can imagine a locality revolving around decentralized and relatively self-sufficient living patterns, representations that imagine the countryside as a diverse home accessible to all, and everyday experiences celebrating the local and the individually meaningful. (Halfacree, 2006, pp. 57–8)

If, as Dan Rebellato suggests, globalisation means that 'patterns of power and injustice extend well beyond the boundaries of nation - while the focus on nation is improperly widened to state level, and the particularity is lost' (2008, p. 254), a focus on the local, and on the specifically rural local, seems to offer an important change of scale and one that is related to the here and now. For Halfacree and Harpin the rural local also seems to offer a potential site for resistance to external structures of (usually capitalist) power; the plays of Churchill and Leyshon add the voices of their own rural locals to this discussion.

The place of performance

This discussion of the rural as represented in performance begins to open up questions about the relationship of what is performed and where it is performed: while Churchill's and Leyshon's work was first performed in the 'local' place, in Colchester and the West Country, the other plays listed by Harpin were all first performed on the stages of London theatres. Returning to the early modern theatre where I began this discussion of 'Performing the rural', Sanders stresses the importance of paying attention to the place and location of audience in a recent essay that considers the place of performance in the context of early modern provincial and rural geographies. In 'Making the Land Known: *Henry IV Parts 1 and 2* and the Literature of Perambulations' (forthcoming) she highlights the changes that were made to performance, when the plays were taken out of the city and into the country, by examining a 1623 production of *Henry IV Parts 1 and 2* adapted by Sir Edward Dering for performance at his country residence, Surrenden in Kent. Sanders notes that Dering excised most of Part 2 including the Gloucestershire scenes, arguing that

> a provincial performance to an insider audience
> with a rather different set of regional knowledges
> and understandings to a London Bankside thea-
> tre might not require the suggestion of the rural
> road networks and cultural and spatial geogra-
> phies of the provinces […] but was instead being
> connected up to the high politics of the capital,
> otherwise transported to them only through
> news and gossip. (Sanders, forthcoming)

But even where such early modern performances took place, exceptionally, in provincial contexts in the halls of country houses, the drama was still being seen from the perspective of the country estate rather than the surrounding fields, forests or mines and the lives lived there. This was landscape as picture and image rather than 'the everyday lives of the rural' in Halfacree's terms. In the final part of this book, then, I turn to look at performances that happen within the rural place, arguing that the creation of performance in and for rural sites comes closest to enabling theatre that remaps and reimagines the rural in productive and challenging ways, suggesting a rethinking of the relationship between theatre and the constituent parts of the nation.

The rural as site for performance

The Company go back to their seats, and read short sections of accounts of the Clearances from many different areas of the North. Note: *readings to be selected from the following, according to where the show is being done.*
READER. 'Donald Sage, Kildonan, Sutherland. The whole inhabitants of Kildonan parish, nearly 2,000 souls, were utterly rooted and burned out. [...]'
READER. Ross-shire. 'From the estate of Robertson of Kindace in the year of 1843 the whole inhabitants of Glencalvie were evicted [...]'

> READER. Strathnaver, Sutherland. 'Grace
> MacDonald took shelter up the brae and
> remained there for a day and a night watching
> the burnings. When a terrified cat jumped from
> a burning cottage it was thrown back in again
> and again until it died'. (John McGrath, *The
> Cheviot, the Stag and the Black, Black Oil*, 1981,
> pp. 16–7)

In 1973, the same year that Williams published *The Country and the City*, 7:84 (Scotland)'s *The Cheviot, the Stag and the Black, Black Oil* began its tour of the Highlands and Islands of Scotland. The production told the story of the repeated and ongoing exploitation of the Scottish Highlands from the original early nineteenth-century Clearances which expelled resident tenant crofters/farmers to create grazing lands for wealthy landowners' Cheviot sheep to the then more recent invasion of the 'international corporations – oil, land, property, building, construction, marine, even catering – [...] jumping about all over the place looking for millions of dollars' in the rapidly expanding North Sea Oil industry (McGrath, 'The Year of the Cheviot', 1981 [1974], p. vii). I want to begin this final section by examining *The Cheviot*'s performance practice, which employed a mixed dramaturgy of popular forms such as music hall, pantomime and the interactive ceilidh music and dance session, in order to argue that theatre and performance taking place *in* the rural offers potentially different relationships to those living and working in the rural, as well as enabling an important space for creativity outside the urban centres.

Like Hamilton and Scullion, McGrath was alert to the mists of both 'romanticism' and 'backwardness' which he argued had shrouded the actual realities of the Highlands, 'created by the actions of a feudal system leaping red in tooth and claw into an imperialist capitalist system' (1981, p. vii). He thus sought to create a style of theatre and to shape a story which would break out of what he saw as the 'lament syndrome' affecting Gaelic culture since the Battle of Culloden in 1746 which represented the last, unsuccessful stand of the Scots against the Hanoverian English kings (p. xxvii). While there was an obvious danger of nostalgia in telling the stories of ancestral resistance to a modern audience separated in time from the realities of past rural lives, *The Cheviot* made use of the specific connections between site, story and performance style to link past to present in place. In the references contained in the extract above to Donald Sage, Grace MacDonald, Robertson of Kindace, Kildonan and Strathnaver 'according to where the show is being done', 7:84 (Scotland) made use of local names and places to create a shared mental and geographical landscape between performance and audience. But here the mention of specific people and places was done not to create a convincing 'mapped reality of place' for an urban audience watching a distant rural, as I have earlier argued is the case in relation to Synge's and McDonagh's Irish plays; rather, the invocation of names and settlements explicitly worked to connect the places being performed to the places of performance, a strategy also reflected in the way that the event carried on either side of the scripted production with songs and a ceilidh to finish the evening. Although the show's first performance took place in the distinctly non-rural setting of Aberdeen Arts Centre, the nights that followed took the company around village halls, dance halls, community centres and schools across the Highlands and Islands, visiting, for example, the harbour village of Kinlochbervie, the old crofting village of Rogart and the seaport of Stromness on Orkney. 7:84's production, like those of Synge's and McDonagh's plays, engaged with the rural history of a nation which had been exploited by outsiders – this time absentee Scottish and English landowners – but it did so on terms that prevented the rural representation being other or alien to its audiences, emphasising a shared space both temporally and geographically. The naming of places was tied to the place of performance, enabling the audience to use the direct connection with place to reach back through time to the individuals who lived there, engaged in a struggle that 7:84 emphasised at the end of the play was a continuing one:

> Remember your hardships and keep up your struggle
> The wheel will turn for you
> By the strength of your hands and hardness of your fists.
> Your cattle will be on the plains
> Everyone in the land will have a place
> And the exploiter will be driven out. (McGrath, 1981, p. 74)

The particular relationship between the represented place of the rural Highlands and the rural place of reception in those same localities in 7:84's *The Cheviot, the Stag and the Black, Black Oil* gave special force to the repeated claim sung – both sincerely and ironically – within the performance that 'These are my mountains'. The sites of performance, together with the ways in which *The Cheviot* worked with ideas of what McGrath has elsewhere called localism of place and localism of material (*A Good Night Out*, 1996, p. 58), protected against nostalgia, suggesting that theatre that is alert to the place of the audience as well as to that of the play's represented place can offer ways of rethinking the rural and of meaningfully engaging with the 'everyday lives' of the people who live and work there.

In such ways, *The Cheviot* can perhaps be seen as an early example of more recent attempts by theatre and performance practitioners to pay attention to the specifics and particularities of place: attention which is fruitful in relation to what I have argued is too often the neglect of rural realities. The writing and performance practice of academic-practitioner Mike Pearson is particularly useful to examine in this context. Always paying close attention to site, and the stories that are generated there, Pearson has worked at a variety of scales from local to national. Working on his own and with others, he has created responses to his childhood landscape of rural Lincolnshire (*Bubbling Tom*, Hibaldstow village, 2000; *Carrlands*, three audio works for the valley of the River Ancholme, North

Lincolnshire, with composers John Hardy and Hugh Fowler, 2007). As collaborator with scenographer Cliff McLucas and others in the Welsh company Brith Gof, he has created site-specific work in response to both the rural and industrial landscape of his adopted Wales (such as *Tri Bywyd* (Three Lives) that took place at an abandoned farm in a conifer plantation, west Wales in 1995 and involved 'Five live performers, including two local actors who had known Esgair Fraith in the 30s and 40s. A dead sheep. Various artifacts including flares, books, buckets of milk, sheets and a pistol'). More recently, with his collaborator Mike Brookes, he has directed a series of site-specific performances for the new National Theatre Wales (*The Persians*, Sennybridge military training range, Brecon Beacons, 2010; *Coriolan/us*, RAF St Athan, Vale of Glamorgan, 2012). With his focus on the local here and the present now, highlighted in his discussion of Doreen Massey's work mentioned earlier, it is perhaps not surprising that *Bubbling Tom*, a solo performance in which Pearson revisited ten key sites in his childhood village, Hibaldstow, took place as one of fourteen performances commissioned by Small Acts at the Millennium in 2000. These aimed 'to create a series of works marking the personal and political resonances of the Millennium and the charged questions it raised, [… creating] a series of actions and site-specific works across the year that were dissident and personal' (Heathfield, 2000). Rather than creating a definitive narrative, *Bubbling Tom* aimed to begin a conversation, a dialogue, with other voices in the rural:

Bubbling Tom is in the form of a leisurely stroll around the village, pausing at ten key points to remember significant events and people in a sequence of performed texts and informal chat.... The following documentation includes some images and fragments of the text for each station. But there is no attempt at completeness here. The document is as fragmentary and partial as the memories which inspired the work, and the memories of the performance work itself, after a couple of days have passed. (Pearson, 2000, p. 176)

Like Churchill and Leyshon, Halfacree and Harpin, Pearson thus operates from an understanding that working with the rural *in* the rural is a key route for enabling the voices and the stories of different rural locals to be heard. What follows is an exploration of approaches to developing and sharing theatre in international and national contexts that increasingly focus on that aim.

From the centre to the rural: theatre for rural development

One area in which the need to incorporate local, rural voices is brought into particularly sharp relief is in the arena of theatre for rural development. Although the majority of this book's focus has been on the rural as both a geographical and a conceptual landscape in the contexts of the United Kingdom and the Republic of Ireland, I have sought to stress that debates about divisions between urban and rural play out in other contexts too. Theatre for Development – otherwise known as Theatre for Integrated Rural Development or Community Theatre for Integrated Rural Development according to Marcia Pompêo Nogueira's 2002 overview of the field in *Research in Drama Education: The Journal of Applied Theatre and Performance* – of course draws on the very different 'legends and landscapes', in Stephen Daniels' terms, of rural settings in developing countries around the world. But the development of such theatre practices and their relationships with rural communities reflect the kinds of concerns that I have already explored in this book and underline the need for an understanding of the rural generated from within rather than from outside that context.

In her discussion of Jana Sanskriti's political theatre in Rural North India, Dia Mohan suggests that 'Rural subjects and their culture are not usually viewed as contemporary producers of the reality we call modernity' (2004, p. 188), noting that 'while rural subjects have access to some cultural spaces, they do not necessarily have control over these spaces or representation in them' (p. 191). But Mohan's ethnographic research in West Bengal, like Ross Kidd's earlier work in Zimbabwe captured in his *From People's Theatre for Revolution to Popular Theatre for Reconstruction: Diary of a Zimbabwean Workshop* (1984), traces a shift in relations between the urban and the rural facilitated by, and played out in the practices of, theatre companies and practitioners working with rural communities. In the context of this volume, I can offer only a brief summary of the history of theatre for rural development. However, the story of progression outlined here – from treating rural audiences as passive objects to working with them as subjects with their own stories to tell – provides an international example of what in this final section I identify as a key issue for rural theatre and performance.

Kidd's useful categorisation of theatre for rural development from the 1950s onwards tracks a change from tours of 'mass education' taking mobile teams of development workers to rural areas with plays on cash crop production, immunisation and sanitation (what Nogueira terms 'theatre as development propaganda', 2002, p. 105), towards an ostensibly democratising practice of taking theatre to the people in the 1960s:

> Groups of university students [from the universities of Ibadan (Nigeria), Makerere (Uganda), Nairobi (Kenya), Malawi and Zambia] took plays on the conflicts between tradition and modernisation and other issues to rural villages [...] as a form of 'cultural democratisation', taking theatre out of the urban enclaves (in which it had operated during the colonial era) and making it accessible to the masses. (Kidd, 1984, p. 5)

Although ostensibly democratising, Nogueira identifies that both such ways of working could be characterised as 'top-down approaches, an imposition of one worldview upon another', and usually, I'd suggest, this imposition comes from the urban to the rural. Nogueira suggests the need for a different approach,

> based on a principle of respect for the actual need of the people not on what we fancy they need. This means that instead of treating rural and urban poor people as objects of development research and projects, they should be treated as subjects (2002, p. 107),

and Kidd and Mohan describe work in Africa and India, respectively, which attempts to do just that, locating theatre in the everyday lives of the rural rather than in the outside perceptions and expectations of governments or development agencies to transformative effect.

> The process created a much more critical perspective, revealing the political-economic roots of the villagers' poverty, landlessness, and unemployment. [...] It also conscientized the development workers, getting them to work *with* rather than *for* the villagers, challenging their developmentalist assumptions and technocratic conditioning, and exposing them to structural perspectives and some of the real constraints faced by peasants. (Kidd, 1984, p. 7, emphasis in original)

Mohan's observation of the Jana Sanskriti theatre organisation emphasises this switch in perspective even more clearly,

noting the development of thirty-five theatre teams in dispa-
rate villages in West Bengal each of which 'combines activity
onstage with activism offstage' (2004, p. 184). By commit-
ting to deep and long-term involvement in rural communities, Mohan argues, Jana Sanskriti enables its members to
'live against the grain of the experiential separations and
order produced through the urban-rural divide' (p. 185).

Rural touring theatre

The village communities of West Bengal and the countries
of Nigeria, Uganda, Kenya, Malawi and Zambia are geographically distant and distinct from the villages or market
towns of the UK. And as I have already stressed, there are
considerable differences between different areas of the rural
UK too. But remarkably similar concerns arise in discussion
of theatre provision for rural audiences and sites in all of
these different rurals. In *A Wider Horizon*, his 2015 study of
Creative Arts East and Rural Touring, Matarasso employs
Jane Jacobs' argument that 'Development cannot be given,
it has to be done. It is a process, not a collection of capital
goods' in support of his argument that rural touring offers a
different model to that of arts development as something to
be given, 'exactly like a collection of artistic goods', that is
suggested by the history of Arts Council activity since the
1940s (Matarasso, 2015, p. 99, citing Jacobs, 1985, p. 119).
Such a rebalancing is perhaps particularly important in the
context of reduced budgets both for arts and local authorities
and in the light of Arts Council England's (ACE) own recent

Rural Evidence and Data Review: Analysis of Arts Council England Investment, Arts and Cultural Participation and Audiences (2015) which notes that while 17.6 per cent of the population of England live in a rural area, only 4.6 per cent of ACE's funded National Portfolio Organisations (NPOs) are based in rural areas, representing just 2.5 per cent of all NPO investment by ACE, some £25.2 million across the three-year funding period 2015–18. Such findings further underline the evidence of a metropolitan funding bias highlighted in the influential 2013 report *Rebalancing Our Cultural Capital: A Contribution to the Debate on National Policy for the Arts and Culture in England* authored by Peter Stark, Christopher Gordon and David Powell. The report acknowledged the positive impacts resulting from initiatives such as the Arts Council's 1984 Glory of the Garden strategy and the more recent Creative People and Places programmes. 'Nevertheless', it concluded, 'in terms of the overall national disposition of resources, the systemic drift of London bias has continued unabated' (2013, p. 15).

Many of the rural-based NPOs funded by ACE will be involved in rural touring, although of course companies based outside the rural may also work there: New Perspectives, the rural touring theatre company for the East Midlands, is currently based in Nottingham, while Eastern Angles, the touring company for the East of England, works from a base in Ipswich. Both are part of a movement that began in the early 1980s when Hampshire County Council established its first rural touring programme in recognition of the need to extend services to take greater account of rural communities; at the same time New Perspectives moved to Mansfield in Nottinghamshire with a specific brief from East Midlands Arts 'to provide a theatre service for village halls, community centres and other venues, particularly in suburban and rural areas, where the opportunities to see live theatre are scarce' (undated press cutting, *Northampton Chronicle*, *The Chimes*, NPT 2/37/1). While the models of delivery have changed across the decades – with touring theatre companies now offering their work to communities via the approximately thirty touring schemes across England that select and in turn offer a range of potential performances to local, volunteer promoters via either a brochure or website – the key elements of rural touring theatre have remained remarkably consistent. Drawing on the work of Matarasso in both *A Wider Horizon* and his earlier book about rural touring, *Only Connect: Arts Touring and Rural Communities* (2004), I want to highlight accessibility, ownership, immediacy and community development and cohesion as those key elements, before briefly examining the practice of New Perspectives in making and touring theatre to the various rurals of England's East Midlands.

In 'The Year of the Cheviot', his introduction to *The Cheviot, the Stag and the Black, Black Oil*, McGrath tells the story of an old Gaelic poet who came up to the company after a performance in the Outer Hebrides to say, 'I have heard the story of my people told with truth'. 'He too', McGrath remarks, 'had been paying taxes to support the Arts Council. For the first time, he was getting something back' (1981, p. xiv). Some thirty years later, a survey undertaken by Matarasso for *Only Connect* similarly highlighted the importance of taking theatre to rural places as part of the overall national provision of theatre and arts development:

> A substantial proportion of the audience does not see live arts except through the touring schemes: about a third of the audience survey respondents (34 per cent) had not attended other events in the previous 12 months. In more remote areas, and among young and older people, this figure is much higher. (2004, p. 11)

Accessibility on its own, however, might still be seen as part of a model of delivery from urban to rural, centre to periphery, which we have seen questioned by both Matarasso and practitioners of theatre for rural development: 'providing a theatre service' to a passive rural consumer. But what is key to rural touring theatre are the additional elements of shared ownership, production and immediacy, which can then facilitate community development.

Across the country, all rural touring schemes work in collaboration with volunteer local promoters who themselves choose the shows. Gavin Stride, current Artistic Director of Farnham Maltings in South East England and former Artistic Director of New Perspectives, comments that 'in village hall touring the promoting, box office, front of house and marketing is undertaken by amateurs in the community – in a highly effective partnership in which the quality of the experience relies equally on maker and audience' ('Arts in rural England', undated). In addition, the performances take place in a space – often the village hall or local primary school – which is more familiar to the audience than to the performers, and in front of an audience who know each other: as Stride asked in his programme for the 2002 New Perspectives' production of *Thank God for Cod*, 'How many opportunities are presented to us [...] *if we make our work in the spaces that people already inhabit?*' (emphasis added). Ownership of place, and co-ownership of event through the touring scheme/volunteer promoter model, can thus be seen to contribute to an immediacy of shared experience that extends beyond the two or three hours of the conventional urban theatre experience to reach into the larger life of the rural community, as Matarasso argues:

> Village hall shows have a great capacity to bring local people together and that aspiration is common among promoters. Audiences span the age range, and include many families; friendship is also important, and people feel comfortable going alone in the expectation of meeting people they know. [...] As arts events, they offer memorable experiences, and can provoke lasting debates, becoming part of the shared history that is a basis of community. (*Only Connect*, 2004, p. 12)

Performing the local rural: New Perspectives as case study

Perhaps as good an example as any of a rural touring theatre show is *Last Stop Louisa's*, written by Amanda Whittington and produced by New Perspectives Theatre Company in 2000 at the company's then base at Mansfield Old Library, north Nottinghamshire, before touring to villages and market towns across the East Midlands' counties at which the company's work was targeted. In many ways the production was nothing particularly out of the ordinary: a comedy drama set on Christmas Eve in one of the run-down transport cafés that still cling to the edges of the A15 highway as it travels across the flatlands of Lincolnshire, it focused on the relationships between the husband and wife owners of the transport café and the gap between their dreams of a life in America and the reality of their own lives on the A15, ultimately celebrating, in the words of the director Martin Wylde, 'those people who stay in a place and work quietly for their community' (*LSL* Programme, NPT 2/92/4).

The production was an utterly routine part of New Perspectives' then established pattern of touring two or three shows a year, always to venues in rural market towns and villages. But *Last Stop Louisa's* can be situated as a particular encounter with regional and rural communities: the play had been specially commissioned with support from the Arts Council 'to celebrate the return of Lincolnshire to the East Midlands in the recent redefining of regional boundaries' and seven new Lincolnshire venues, including Hougham & Marston Village Hall and the Moulton Community Centre, Spalding, were added to those already established as potential locations for New Perspectives' work (*LSL* programme, 2000). Quoted in the press release publicising the production, Stride was clear about the play's – and the company's – relationship to place, region and the rural, arguing that '*Last Stop Louisa's* has the mud of Lincolnshire on its boots but the issues of the play are pertinent to most people who have grown up or live in rural areas' (*LSL* Press release, 2000).

In some ways, offering a specific example is unhelpful here, as it is the practice and model of rural touring theatre to which I want to call the reader's attention, rather than the content of any particular play. That is not to say that the content is not important, or that the rural touring theatre model does not enable a particularly fruitful exploration of rural themes with rural audiences: the company highlighted in the *Last Stop Louisa's* programme that it was

> driven by a desire to create work that is rooted in the particularity of the communities of the region with most of the plays being commissioned new works from writers who have an car and an eye to the concerns and aspirations of local people.

I might also mention here, for example, New Perspectives' 2007 *On Saturdays this Bed is Poland*, about which the *Guardian*'s Brian Logan noted that

> while recent plays have tackled the railways, the police, the prison service and the war, theatre's radar has yet to register the arrival in the UK

> of up to one million eastern European migrant
> workers. Now the subject is to be addressed,
> not by the National or the Royal Court, but by
> a rural touring outfit in the east Midlands. ('Oh
> my God, this is my life', 26 April 2007)

The play aimed to get audiences talking about issues
that directly affected their community: the then Artistic
Director Daniel Buckroyd noted that 'People will gather
and talk about these issues. Individually and collectively,
their feelings about what's going on in their locale will
change. We want to provide the impetus for those communities to have a great night out and engage'. More recently
still, the company's 2013 *Entertaining Angels*, written by
Brendan Murray, was commissioned to look at the role
of the Church of England in rural village life. But New
Perspectives are also aware that their practice of touring
theatre works beyond the content of any particular evening's performance, and are very alert to the importance
of a good or great night out: recent research undertaken
with promoters by the company's rural touring scheme
Northants Touring Arts (NTA) highlighted that for one
promoter at least,

> I'm not convinced that rural issues are really a
> draw to rural audiences. We expend consider-
> able amounts of effort combating encroaching
> urbanization so these issues are not necessar-
> ily entertainment! I suppose we are looking for

performances that stretch our experiences or transport us to worlds that we have never contemplated and sometimes we are just looking for a laugh! (Information from NTA, personal email)

Set against the model of theatre for rural development outlined by Nogueira, we might note that rural touring theatre, while taking theatre to the rural and often making theatre about the rural, does not always involve active participation by the rural. However, Matarasso argues that

Rural touring has often been the first step in local arts and community development initiatives, valuable because it is accessible, yet demanding. People in villages like Terrington (Yorkshire), Bergh Apton (Norfolk) and Ashbrittle (Somerset), have used touring to develop new community projects and organizations, with positive outcomes for rural cohesion and regeneration. (*Only Connect*, 2004, p. 12)

In the 1990s and early 2000s New Perspectives developed their own models of community participation, working to develop community arts activities at various sites across the East Midland region, including 1999's *Let's Go, Little Darling*, written by Richard Pinner, which was a co-production with seven local amateur theatre groups with the 'aim to create new opportunities for people to take part in the performing arts locally'. More recently, a collaborative research project undertaken with New Perspectives from 2012–15 by Mathilda Branson, 'Re-imagining the rural tour', has explored different ways of enabling interaction and participation among a village hall audience in the context of a rural touring economy that means the company tours to different villages and different rural areas each night.

In a wider sense of creating shared experiences, what underpins this brief case study of New Perspectives' work and of rural touring theatre more generally is an understanding that through its model of shared ownership and place, rural touring shows can work not just to give communities a voice but also to contribute to the very building of those communities, suggesting a different relationship between theatre, representation and audience in rural settings. In Matarasso's words in *A Wider Horizon*,

> In gathering for the evening in the village hall for an event that they or their neighbours have organised, people affirm not just their cultural tastes and values but also their willingness to be a community in the first place. In all my conversations with people about rural touring, over more than ten years now, the most consistent reason they give for being involved is that it brings the community together. Whether they are promoters, neighbours or incomers, the people who turn up on a cold night to see an unknown play

by an equally unfamiliar theatre group do so to support the community. And, of course, the best way to promote our values is to enact them. It's not what we say but what we do that makes a difference. (2015, p. 94)

Defining new nationals through theatre: including the rural

Such an approach has, I'd argue, been central to the developing work of the two new national theatres of the United Kingdom, the National Theatre of Scotland (first performances 2006) and the National Theatre Wales (first performances 2010), in terms of 'doing' what it might mean to be national through practice that draws explicitly on a rural touring model rather than just 'saying' a company is national, in Matarasso's terms. Both companies are theatres without buildings, with 'no bricks-and-mortar institutionalism to counter, nor the security of a permanent home in which to develop', in the words of the manifesto pledge of Vicky Featherstone, first director of the National Theatre of Scotland. As a result, both theatres have made a virtue of creating theatre and meeting audiences across the diverse landscapes and buildings of their respective home countries.

The National Theatre of Scotland's first performance, *Home* (February 2006), was located not just in one place or even just in the cities and major conurbations of Scotland but rather in ten separate venues across the country, including its Highlands and Islands, and consisted of ten different shows, each of which responded to the particular place, its history and stories. So while *Home Aberdeen* (directed by Alison Peebles) was staged in a derelict tenement block in that city, *Home East Lothian* (directed by Gill Robertson) took its family audiences deep into a forest to explore the story of Hansel and Gretel, *Home Stornoway* (directed by Stewart Laing) took place in a disused shop in the town centre on this Hebridean island and *Home Shetland* (directed by Wils Wilson) was staged on the car deck of the Northlink Ferry in Lerwick Harbour. Travelling between the city of Aberdeen and the Shetland Islands, the ferry became a particularly resonant site for a performance which Roger Cox identified as exploring the 'perennial island tension between leaving and staying', perhaps exemplifying the sense that in the contemporary world rural and urban are not separated, but always interlinked with each other ('For one weekend, all the world's a stage – or all the country, at least', *The Scotsman*, 27 February 2006). As Trish Reid comments in her article, '"From scenes like these old Scotia's grandeur springs": The New National Theatre of Scotland', 'Wilson's production played with the conflicting meanings of the ferry as representing both leaving and returning, conflating these meanings to construct a Shetland identity significantly defined by its many partings and reunions' (2007, p. 199).

The National Theatre of Scotland describes its mission as 'mak[ing] theatre wherever we can connect with an audience – a promise we take seriously. Our work has been shown in airports and high-rises, forests and ferries, drill halls and football pitches, pubs and factories'. Central to this, as Ben Walmsley makes clear, is the company's engagement in rural touring, which brings with it not only the 'art of closeness' in Matarasso's terms but also the ability to reach all geographical areas of the Scotland which the theatre aims to represent:

> There are several reasons why rural touring is so important to NTS: Firstly, as the national theatre company in Scotland, it accepts it has an explicit duty to produce and tour work all over the country; secondly, it acknowledges that people living in rural communities are just as entitled to high quality theatre as their compatriots in Edinburgh or Glasgow; and thirdly, it values the artistic, social and audience development opportunities unique to rural touring. (2010, p. 114)

To Walmsley's lists of benefits I would add a final point, beyond a focus on widening audience reach. In taking theatre to the rural as well as the urban, and in *making* theatre in the rural as well as the urban, the National Theatre of Scotland is better placed to tell the stories of *all* of Scotland, stories that are dependent on lived experience of place, and which grow from the everyday lives of the rural as well the more usual urban contexts of theatre making.

This is also true of the National Theatre Wales, launched in 2010, which shares much of its Scottish counterpart's approach to making theatre across the full range of its country's geography, rural and urban, as it makes explicit in its claim that 'The nation of Wales is our stage: From forests to beaches, from aircraft hangars to post-industrial towns, village halls to nightclubs':

> We work all over the country, and beyond, using Wales' rich and diverse landscape, its towns, cities and villages, its incredible stories and rich talent as our inspiration.

> Our audiences have followed us and Michael Sheen like disciples around his hometown, Port Talbot, to watch *The Passion*. Some partied with Neon Neon (Gruff Rhys & Boom Bip) in Cardiff, learning the extraordinary story of Italian publisher Giangiacomo Feltrinelli, in *Praxis Makes Perfect*. Hundreds climbed the foothills of Snowdon to hear poems by the national poet of Wales, Gillian Clarke and witness first-hand the annual sheep-gathering. Many watched a marathon, overnight performance of *Iliad* in Llanelli. Others donned wellies to experience *Mametz*, written by poet Owen Sheers and staged in farmland near Usk, and which offered a chilling glimpse of life and death in a WWI trench.

Explicit here is a commitment not just to take theatre out of the urban into the rural but instead to tell the stories of many different locals, the rural as well as the urban, developing those stories from place and in place. The performance in the foothills of Snowdon, *The Gathering/Yr Helfa*, for example, was the culmination of three years' observation of life at Hafod y Llan, a working hill farm on the mountain. Lyn Gardner's review for the *Guardian* highlights the key elements of place and story as organically interlinked and developed together, describing the performance as

> an intervention in a landscape yet [one that] grows organically from its setting, using what is there – the abandoned dwellings and slate, the waterfalls and rocks – to tell a story of passing time, ancient ways of working, extraordinary fecundity and renewal, but also bitter barrenness. It's lyrical but unsentimental, bloody and brutal. It makes the mountain sing. ('*The Gathering* review – sheep are the stars in Snowdon theatre show', *Guardian*, 15 September 2014)

And while the forests, mountains and beaches of Wales have formed the backdrop to company shows such as *The Beach* (Prestatyn, July 2010), *For Mountain, Sand and Sea* (Barmouth, June 2010) and *Branches: The Nature of Crisis* (Flintshire, September 2012), National Theatre Wales has been careful not to place rural work only in the romanticised rural of our conventional imagination but also in the metaphorical abattoirs and the actual pit villages that, as I have tried to stress throughout this book, are just as much part of the non-urban. Their launch performance, *A Good Night Out in the Valleys* (March 2010), was staged in Miners' Institutes and Workmen's Halls across the South Wales valleys, from Blackwood (population 23,380) to Blaengarw (1,789). Reviewer Quentin Letts wrote,

> Amid jokes about the mobile phone reception in the Valleys and the meatiness of the Welsh diet – a raffle prize from a butcher's is described as 'basically a whole farmyard in a box' – there is honest reflection about the tedium of life there. ('Miner's tale has struck gold in the Valleys', *Daily Mail*, 19 March 2010)

And in all cases, as with 7:84, the work of the rural touring schemes and the productions of the National Theatre of Scotland, the company is concerned that their rural sites of performance should not be seen as stuck in the past but as integrally connected to the present. *A Good Night Out in the Valleys* was, in the words of one reviewer, a

> slice-of-life play [that] cuts deep as well as wide, playing the dysfunction of contemporary post-industrial life against a deep-seated awareness of the past [...] in a nation now ready to engage with its future as well as its past. ('A Good Night Out in the Valleys', *Wales Arts Review*, 16 December 2012)

Conclusion

Through its examination of theatre about the rural and theatre performed in the rural, this book has argued that theatre makers need to be alert to the persistence of romanticised or backward 'cultural mappings' that Cloke suggests may 'precede and direct the recognition of rural space, presenting us with some kind of virtual rurality' (2006, p. 22). With the ability to move beyond fixed and static landscapes and to mobilise the bodies of actors, performers and storytellers in rural place, theatre has a key role to play in both producing and potentially changing understandings of the rural; at the same time, performances in the rural have an important part to play in sharing art and culture with the widest possible audience.

However, from the initial discussion of Williams' *The Country and the City* onwards, I have also been concerned to highlight the dangers and problems of a divide in understanding or representation between the urban and the rural. While this book's focus on the rural has necessitated a concentration on rural themes and rural performances, I am conscious of the danger of simply re-staging or re-stating that divide from a reverse perspective: I hope that *Theatre & the Rural* will take its place on the bookshelves alongside the books in this series titled *Theatre & the City* (by Jen Harvie) and *Theatre & Nation* (by Nadine Holdsworth) in a spirit of interconnectedness and recalibration rather than separation.

In arguing here for the importance of understanding how particular spatial and cultural imaginaries of the rural can neglect and silence the realities of the everyday lives lived in rural communities in the UK and around the globe, I have drawn on an understanding of localities and places as continually produced by a variety of different forces and impulses, among them the cultural representations of theatre and performance, and therefore have repeatedly acknowledged that there is not one rural but rather many different rurals. In optimistic conclusion to this book, with its plea for theatre to look again at the rural, the work of the two new national theatres seems to be attempting to bridge – or perhaps to transgress or break down – the divide between urban and rural, including the everyday and the local lives of all landscapes within their reach. In doing so, they draw on a model familiar to rural touring theatre of localism and closeness, and pay attention to the stories of the pragmatic everyday lives of the rural, 'fractured and inco-herent' as all lives are in reality. 'Poverty in an age of afflu-ence is being unable to write and have others write about you', said Michael Simmons' interviewee in *Landscapes of Poverty: Aspects of Rural England in the Late 1990s* (1997, p. 157). My hope is that this volume will encourage readers to begin to listen to the many and varied voices of the rural, and to rethink the ways in which theatre might enable the creation of new rural imaginaries.

further reading

Michael Woods' *Rural* (2011), written for students of human geography, provides a useful introduction to definitions of the rural and highlights the importance of 'rural space as central to many key issues facing contemporary society'. As a critical geography textbook, it does not address theatre and dramatic performance either in or about the rural, but it does examine the production and reproduction of the diverse meanings that have been attached to the rural, and shows the influence of those meanings in shaping the everyday lives of people who live, work or play there. Critical reading in cultural studies and social geography that underpins my approach to the place of the rural includes Cresswell, Harvey, Lefebvre, Massey and Crang and Thrift. Williams' *The City and the Country* (1973) provides a potential model for an extended treatment of literature's engagement with the concepts of, and relationship between, the city and the country from the seventeenth century onwards, but apart from a brief consideration of Jacobean and Restoration comedy, Williams pays little attention to the representation of the country or the rural in theatre and performance. Frye's useful concept of the 'green world' drama has been widely applied to early modern drama but less attention has been paid to modern and contemporary engagements with the rural beyond discussion of individual writers and plays. Here I have drawn on Pearson's work on site-specific performance, regionality and the rural, and also drawn on a number of reports written for and about the rural touring sector, particularly by Matarasso.

Anon. *The Towneley Second Shepherds' Play*. Norton Anthology of English Literature, Vol. 1. 8th edn. 2005.

Arts Council England. *Rural Evidence and Data Review: Analysis of Arts Council England Investment, Arts and Cultural Participation and Audiences*. Manchester: Arts Council England, 2015.

Aston, Elaine. *Caryl Churchill*. 2nd edn. Tavistock: Northcote House, 2001.

Balme, Christopher. *Cambridge Introduction to Theatre Studies*. Cambridge: Cambridge University Press, 2008.

Bevington, David. 'Introduction'. *As You Like It*. Internet Shakespeare Edition and Broadview Press, University of Victoria, 2012.

Bond, Edward. *Bingo: Scenes of Money and Death. Plays: 3*. London: Methuen, 1999.

Bonnett, Alastair. *Left in the Past: Radicalism and the Politics of Nostalgia*. New York: Bloomsbury Publishing, 2010.

Bouchard, Michel Marc. *Tom at the Farm*. Trans. Linda Gaboriau. Vancouver: Talonbooks, 2013.

Butterworth, Jez. *Jerusalem*. London: Nick Hern Books, 2009.

Carlson, Marvin. *Places of Performance: The Semiotics of Theatre Architecture*. Ithaca: Cornell University Press, 1993.

Casey, Edward. *Getting Back into Place: Toward a Renewed Understanding of the Place-World*. Bloomington and Indianapolis: Indiana University Press. 2nd edn. 2009.

Churchill, Caryl. *Light Shining in Buckinghamshire*. *Plays: One*. London: Methuen, 1985.

————. *Fen*. *Plays: Two*. London: Methuen, 1990.

Clarke, Brenna Katz. *The Emergence of the Peasant Play at the Abbey Theatre*. Ann Arbor: UMI Research Press, 1982.

Cloke, Paul. 'Conceptualizing Rurality'. *Handbook of Rural Studies*, eds. Paul Cloke, Terry Marsden and Patrick Mooney. London: Sage, 2006. 18–28.

Cloke, Paul, P. Milbourne and C. Thomas. *Lifestyles in Rural England: A Research Report to the Department of the Environment, the Economic and Social Research Council and the Rural Development Commission*. Rural Development Commission, 1994.

Cochrane, Claire. *Twentieth Century Theatre: Industry, Art and Empire*. Cambridge: Cambridge University Press, 2011.

Crang, Mike and Nigel J. Thrift. *Thinking Space*. London: Routledge, 2000.

Cresswell, Tim. *Place: A Short Introduction*. Oxford: Blackwell, 2004.

Daniels, Stephen. *Fields of Vision: Landscape Imagery and National Identity in England and the United States*. Cambridge: Polity Press, 1993.

DEFRA (Department for Environment, Food & Rural Affairs, UK). *The Rural–Urban Classification for England*. 2013.

Eyre, Richard and Nicholas Wright. *Changing Stages: A View of British Theatre in the Twentieth Century*. London: Bloomsbury, 2000.

Frye, Northrop. *Anatomy of Criticism: Four Essays*. Princeton, NJ: Princeton University Press, 1957.

Grene, Nicolas. *The Politics of Irish Drama: Plays in Context from Boucicault to Friel*. Cambridge: Cambridge University Press, 1999.

Halfacree, Keith. 'Rural Space: Constructing a Three-fold Architecture'. *Handbook of Rural Studies*, eds. Paul Cloke, Terry Marsden and Patrick Mooney. London: Sage, 2006. 44–62.

Hamilton, Christine and Adrienne Scullion. *The Same, but Different: Rural Arts Touring in Scotland – The Case of Theatre*. Stroud: Comedia, 2004.

Harpin, Anna. 'Land of Hope and Glory: Jez Butterworth's Tragic Landscapes'. *Studies in Theatre and Performance*, 31.1 (2011), 61–73.

Harvie, Jen. *Staging the UK*. Manchester: Manchester University Press, 2005.

Heathfield, Adrian, ed. *Small Acts: Performance, the Millennium and the Marking of Time*. London: Black Dog, 2000.

Hilton, Rodney Howard. *The English Peasantry in the Later Middle Ages: The Ford Lectures for 1973, and Related Studies*. Oxford: Clarendon, 1975.

Hughes, Declan. 'Who The Hell Do We Think We Are? Reflections on Irish Theatre and Identity'. *Theatre Stuff: Critical Essays on Contemporary Irish Theatre*, ed. Eamonn Jordan. Dublin: Carysfort, 2009. 8–15.

Innes, Christopher. *Modern British Drama: 1890–1980*. Cambridge: Cambridge University Press, 1992.

Jacobs, Jane. *Cities and the Wealth of Nations: Principles of Economic Life*. Harmondsworth: Viking, 1985.

Kerrigan, John. 'Henry IV and the Death of Old Double'. *Essays in Criticism*, 40.1 (1990), 24–53.

Kidd, Ross. *From People's Theatre for Revolution to Popular Theatre for Reconstruction: Diary of a Zimbabwean Workshop*. The Hague/Toronto: Centre for the Study of Education in Developing Countries, 1984.

Kingsley-Smith, Jane. *Shakespeare's Drama of Exile*. Basingstoke: Palgrave Macmillan, 2003.

Kingsnorth, Paul. *Real England: The Battle Against the Bland*. London: Portobello, 2008.

Kiser, Lisa J. '"Mak's Heirs": Sheep and Humans in the Pastoral Ecology of the Towneley First and Second Shepherds' Plays'. *Journal of English and Germanic Philology*, 108.3 (2009), 336–59.

Lefebvre, Henri. *The Production of Space*. Trans. Donald Nicholson Smith. Oxford: Blackwell, 1991. Original edition published 1974.

Leyshon, Nell. *The Farm*. London: Oberon Books, 2002.

Lonergan, Patrick. 'Martin McDonagh, Globalization and Irish Theatre Criticism'. *The Theatre of Martin McDonagh: A World of Savage Stories*, eds. Lillian Chambers and Eamonn Jordan. Dublin: Carysfort, 2006. 295–323.

Mangan, Michael. *Edward Bond*. Exeter: Northcote House, 1998.

Massey, Doreen. *For Space*. London: Sage, 2005.

Matarasso, François. *Only Connect: Arts Touring and Rural Communities*. Stroud: Comedia, 2004.

Matarasso, François with Rosie Redzia. *A Wider Horizon*. Wymondham: Creative Arts East, 2015.

McGrath, John. *The Cheviot, the Stag and the Black, Black Oil*. London: Methuen, 1981 [1974].

——. *A Good Night Out: Popular Theatre: Audience, Class and Form*. 2nd edn. London: Nick Hern Books, 1996.

Mohan, Dia. 'Reimagining Community: Scripting Power and Changing the Subject Through Jana Sanskriti's Political Theatre in Rural North India'. *Journal of Contemporary Ethnography*, 33.2 (2004), 178–217.

Mormont, Marc. 'Who is Rural? Or, How to be Rural: Towards a Sociology of the Rural'. *Rural Restructuring: Global Processes and Their Responses*, eds. Terry Marsden, Philip Lowe and Sarah Whatmore. London: David Fulton, 1990. 21–44.

Murdoch, Jonathan and Andy C. Pratt. 'Rural Studies: Modernism, Postmodernism and the "Post-Rural"'. *Journal of Rural Studies*, 9.4 (1993), 411–27.

New Perspectives Theatre Company Archive. University of Nottingham, Department of Manuscripts and Special Collections.

Nogueira, Marcia Pompêo. 'Theatre for Development: An Overview'. *Research in Drama Education: The Journal of Applied Theatre and Performance*, 7:1 (2002), 103–8.

O'Toole, Fintan. 'Going West: The Country Versus the City in Irish Writing'. *The Crane Bag*, 9.2 (1985), 111–16.

Pearson, Mike. '*Bubbling Tom*'. *Small Acts: Performance, the Millennium and the Marking of Time*, ed. Adrian Heathfield. London: Black Dog, 2000. 172–85.

——. *Site-Specific Performance*. Basingstoke: Palgrave Macmillan, 2010.

Pilkington, Lionel. *Theatre & Ireland*. Basingstoke: Palgrave Macmillan, 2010.

Rabey, David Ian. *David Rudkin: Sacred Disobedience: An Expository Study of His Drama 1959–1994*. Amsterdam: Harwood, 1997.

——. *The Theatre and Films of Jez Butterworth*. London: Bloomsbury, 2015.

Rabillard, Sheila. 'On Caryl Churchill's Ecological Drama: Right to Poison the Wasps?'. *The Cambridge Companion to Caryl Churchill*, eds. Elaine Aston and Elin Diamond. Cambridge: Cambridge University Press, 2009. 88–104.

Rebellato, Dan. 'From the State of the Nation to Globalization: Shifting Political Agendas in Contemporary British Playwriting'. *A Concise Companion to Contemporary British and Irish Drama*, eds. Nadine Holdsworth and Mary Luckhurst. Oxford: Blackwell, 2008, 245–62.

Reid, Trish. '"From Scenes Like These Old Scotia's Grandeur Springs": The New National Theatre of Scotland'. *Contemporary Theatre Review*, 17:2 (2007), 192–201.

Richards, Shaun. '"The Outpouring of a Morbid, Unhealthy Mind": The Critical Condition of Synge and McDonagh'. *The Theatre of Martin McDonagh: A World of Savage Stories*, eds. Lillian Chambers and Eamonn Jordan. Dublin: Carysfort, 2006. 246–63.

Rose, Gillian. 'Place and Identity: A Sense of Place'. *A Place in the World: Places, Cultures and Globalisation*, eds. Doreen Massey and Pat Jess. Oxford: Oxford University Press, 1995. 87–132.

Rudkin, David. *Afore Night Come. New English Dramatists: 7.* Harmondsworth: Penguin, 1963.

Rural Development Commission. *Lifestyles in Rural England.* 1994.

Sanders, Julie. *The Cambridge Introduction to Early Modern Drama, 1576– 1642.* Cambridge: Cambridge University Press, 2014.

———. 'Making the Land Known: *Henry IV Parts 1 and 2* and the Literature of Perambulations'. Forthcoming.

Scottish Government. *Scottish Government Urban/Rural Classification 2013–2014.* 2014.

Scullion, Adrienne. 'Pastoral Drama'. *The Oxford Encyclopedia of Theatre and Performance*, ed. Dennis Kennedy. Oxford: Oxford University Press, 2010.

Shakespeare, William. *As You Like It*. ed. Juliet Dusinberre. Arden Shakespeare. London: Bloomsbury, 2006 [c.1599].

Simmons, Michael. *Landscapes of Poverty: Aspects of Rural England in the Late 1990s.* London: Lemos and Crane, 1997.

Stark, Peter, Christopher Gordon and David Powell. *Rebalancing Our Cultural Capital: A Contribution to the Debate on National Policy for the Arts and Culture in England.* 2013.

Stride, Gavin. 'Arts in Rural England'. http://gavinstride.co.uk/articles/. Accessed 16 November 2015.

Varbanova, Lidia. 'Developing and Revitalizing Rural Communities Through Arts and Creativity: EUROPE'. Prepared for the Creative City Network of Canada, 2009. http://www.creativecity.ca/database/files/library/rural_communities_arts_2009.pdf.

Walmsley, Ben. 'National Theatre of Scotland and its Sense of Place'. *Marketing Review*, 10.2 (2010), 109–17.

Waters, Steve. *The Secret Life of Plays*. London: Nick Hern Books, 2010.

Welsh Statistical Directorate. SB10/2008: *'Rural Wales' – Definitions and How to Choose Between Them*. 2008.

Wesker, Arnold. *The Wesker Trilogy: Chicken Soup with Barley/Roots/I'm Talking about Jerusalem*. Harmondsworth: Penguin, 1964.

Williams, Raymond. *The Country and the City*. London: Chatto & Windus, 1973.

Wilmer, S.E. *Theatre, Society and Nation: Staging American Identities*. Cambridge: Cambridge University Press, 2002.

Woods, Michael. *Rural*. London: Routledge, 2011.

index

7:84 (Scotland), 54–57, 78
Abbey Theatre, Dublin, 40–1
Arts Council England, 63–4

Blake, William, 'Jerusalem', 1, 7
Bond, Edward, *Bingo: Scenes of
Money and Death*, 29–30
Bouchard, Michel Marc, *Tom à la
ferme* (Tom at the Farm), 37–8
Brith Gof, *Tri Bywyd* (Three
Lives), 58
Brome, Richard, *A Jovial Crew*, 23, 27
Butterworth, Jez,
Jerusalem, 1–3, 5, 6, 7, 8, 21,
26–27, 28, 35, 50
The Night Heron, 50

Chautauqua gatherings, 11
Churchill, Caryl, 59
Fen, 9–10, 46–9, 51–2
*Light Shining in
Buckinghamshire*, 23

Countryside Commission, 16
Cresswell, Tim, 13, 19

Delaney, Shelagh, *A Taste of
Honey*, 31
Dering, Sir Edward, 52
Diggers, 23, 29
drama of the green world, 23–24,
27–28, 29–30, 42, 47

everyday lives of the rural, 14, 34,
44–7, 53, 57, 62, 75, 79–80

Frye, Northrop,
see drama of the green world

globalisation, 47, 49–50, 51
and relationship to rural local,
9, 50–51

Halfacree, Keith, 10, 13–15, 29,
34, 50–1, 53, 59

Irish Literary Theatre, 40
Irish National Dramatic
    Company, 40

Lefebvre, Henri, 4, 14, 18–9, 42
    conceived space, 14–5,
        25, 29, 44
    lived space, 14–5, 44
    perceived space, 14–5
Levellers, 23
Leyshon, Nell, 45–6, 51, 59
    Comfort Me with Apples, 50
    The Farm, 46–9
localism, 57, 80

Massey, Doreen, 44–5
Matarasso, François,
    Only Connect, 10, 13, 16, 65–6,
        67, 71, 75
    A Wider Horizon, 63, 65, 72–3
McDonagh, Martin, 40–4, 55, 56
    The Beauty Queen of Leenane, 41
    The Lieutenant of Inishmore, 41
McGrath, John,
    *The Cheviot, the Stag and the
        Black Black Oil*, 53–7, 65
    A Good Night Out, 57
Murray, Brendan, *Entertaining
    Angels*, 70

National Theatre of Scotland, 73–5
    Home, 73–4
National Theatre Wales, 73, 75–78
    The Gathering / Yr Helfa, 76–7
    *A Good Night Out in the
        Valleys*, 77–8

New Perspectives Theatre
    Company, 68–73
Northants Touring Arts, 70–1
nostalgia, 18, 50, 57
    nostalgic perspective on the
        rural, 3, 18–20, 45, 50–1,
        55, 57

Osborne, John, *Look Back in Anger*, 31

pastoral, definition, 20–21
Pearson, Mike, 44–5, 57–9
    Bubbling Tom, 57–9
    Carrlands, 57–8
    Tri Bywyd, 58
Pinner, Richard, *Let's Go Little
    Darling*, 71–2

Rudkin, David, *Afore Night Come*,
    35–7, 41, 44
rural,
    definitions of, 9–11
    threefold model of, 14–5
    rural-urban classification, 11–12
    as multiple, 3, 13, 76–7, 79–80
    as divided from the urban, 4,
        11–12, 16–17, 20, 59–60,
        63, 79
    as representative of national
        identity, 26, 38–9, 40, 41–4
    as other, 7, 34, 25, 30, 31–8,
        43–4, 45
    as a place of exile, 22, 25, 26–30
    as landscape of the mind, 12–3
    as radical space, 50–1
Rural Development Commission, 16

rural touring theatre, 64–73, 75
   companies as National Portfolio
   Organisations (NPOs), 64

Towneley *First Shepherds' Play*, 8
Towneley *Second Shepherds' Play*,
   5–7, 8, 20

Shakespeare, William,
   A Midsummer Night's Dream, 23,
     24, 27
   As You Like It, 21–2, 23, 24, 25,
     26, 27
   Henry IV Part 1, 52
   Henry IV Part 2, 24–6, 52
Shirley, James, *The Sisters*, 23
space as produced, 4, 13, 19, 44–5,
   79
Synge, John Millington, 40, 43,
   55, 56
   The Playboy of the Western World,
     40–2

theatre for rural development,
   60–3

   also theatre for integrated rural
     development
   also community theatre for
     integrated rural
     development
   in West Bengal, 60, 62–3
   in Africa, 60–62
   as top down approach, 61–2

Wesker, Arnold,
   Chicken Soup with Barley, 31
   *I'm Talking About
     Jerusalem*, 27–9
   Roots, 31–5
Whittington, Amanda, *Last Stop
   Louisa's*, 68–69
Wilkinson, Julie, *On Saturdays this
   Bed is Poland*, 69–70
Williams, Raymond, *The Country
   and the City*, 3–4, 16–7, 18,
   20, 21, 35, 54, 79
Wycherley, William, *The Country
   Wife*, 32

acknowledgements

This book would not exist without the inspiration of my collaborative partners at New Perspectives Theatre Company, the rural touring theatre company for the East Midlands region: artistic director Jack McNamara, chief executive Sally Tye, and my UK Arts and Humanities Research Council-funded collaborative doctoral student, Mathilda Branson, who has been exploring the challenges of enhancing audience engagement in the context of touring rural theatre. Past staff at New Perspectives – Gavin Stride, Daniel Buckroyd and Chris Kirkwood – also inspired me to look more closely at the rural as a site for performance. At the University of Nottingham, Julie Sanders and Jim Moran have been enthusiastic supporters of this project, and Janette Dillon and Mike Jones have generously shared their knowledge. The University of Nottingham's Department of Manuscripts and Special Collections supported an exhibition on regional theatre that helped me develop some of the ideas explored here. I am very grateful to Jen Harvie and the team at Palgrave, including the anonymous reviewer, for insightful editorial support.

Thanks finally to Nick Robinson, who is never afraid to ask a challenging question, but always helps me to find the answer.